Praise for K

"It is the best of its kind
Autobiography of a Yogi."

Adrian Gilbert - Author of 'Blood of Avalon' and 'The Holy Kingdom'

"Superbly written, deeply emotional and empowering, this trilogy is a delightful gift and a powerful testament of wisdom, self-belief, courage, determination and uncommon grace. Joshi's vivid and honest account of her troubled and brave childhood in India, adolescence in London and her remarkable journeys through holy sites and *ashrams* is breathtaking and will keep you engrossed. Her lack of bitterness at the traumatic experiences she encountered as a child and how she overcame her life traumas of self-knowledge and actualisation is truly inspiring and healing, and will surely help others to overcome theirs."

MonaLisa Chukwuma - Author of 'Define Yourself - and Become the Architect of your Future'

"Smita is a bridge and guide for anyone who is on their journey back to the inner light source consciousness within us all. She opens the depth of her own diverse experience to mine the jewels, the pearls of wisdom that is an offering to the modern world from the roots."

Shiva Rea - Master Yoga Teacher and Author of 'Tending the Heart Fire'

"The path to greater self-awareness and understanding that brings us happiness can be rocky and, at times, even treacherous. Smita has been there and got the T-shirt and came back to share the gems of wisdom so that you don't have to do it the hard way. In the *Karma & Diamonds* trilogy, Smita shows how the happiness and fulfilment that we seek are often closer to home than we think. Her account is as entertaining as it is frank. Prepare to ride a roller coaster with her."

Tom Evans - Author of 'New Magic for a New Era'

"A page turner with a difference. Smita Joshi has given us an absorbing, heart-warming and inspirational account of how it's indeed possible, with vision and self-belief, to rise above the challenges of life and succeed with gusto.

Karma & Diamonds is a gripping trilogy about the struggles of a courageous woman conquering the challenges life throws at her. A whirlwind storyline packed with travel, action and emotion, it is often funny but will drive most of us to tears as we identify with the characters and witness many tragic events Smita gets confronted with. Yet, her journey is inspiring and optimistic."

Arvind Devalia - Author of the Amazon bestseller 'Get the Life you Love'

"Without ever preaching, Smita inspires and enlightens the reader to connect to their own inner Self and live life fulfilled. She shows how it's possible to collaborate with the inner Self, even in the most dire of circumstances, to create powerful, wholesome outcomes. Read it as just an engrossing story or allow its deeper messages to alter you forever. One thing is for sure, you will not escape being touched and blown away by this unique story."

Chris Day - Author of 'Turning your Knowledge into Income'

"In this series of books, Smita Joshi has gifted us with an opportunity to follow the struggles of a young British Indian girl as she navigates family tragedy and upheaval, deep traditional expectations and massive inter-cultural differences - whilst at the same time fighting a never-ending battle to trace her own unique path into womanhood, financial success and spiritual freedom.

It is a gem of a tale to inspire all those seeking to transcend limitation, both inner and outer, and all those seeking to become the ultimate source of their own truth and power."

Robert Thé - Anthropologist

"Along the path of Karma yoga, action with selfless intention, Smita has truly have found a light that will never go out."

Stewart Gilchrist - Master Yoga Teacher

"I loved the *Karma & Diamonds* trilogy. This is a heart-warming and true-to-life account of the life and spiritual journey of a brave and determined young British Indian woman.

Book One, *Moon Child*, chronicles Smita's life from a trauma in early childhood to the difficult move from India to England in her early teens, and on into young adulthood, where she realises that to find any peace she has to take a huge leap into the unknown.

Book Two, *Web of Karma*, follows Smita as a young woman on a spiritual journey who also has to develop and grow within a cut-throat and male-dominated business arena. She has to learn how to synchronise her inner spiritual life with the outer mundane one. In this book, Smita faces her demons not only from this life, but from past existences too. At the end of all this, she then finds herself with a life-threatening illness to deal with.

Book Three, *Diamond Revealed*, shows Smita's steady spiritual growth and physical recovery as she becomes more in tune with what she calls her 'Inner Diamond'. Just when she thought her life was predictable, love comes her way. She now has to learn to navigate this new aspect to life, while continuing to integrate the mundane with the spiritual. Old doubts spring up, and Smita has to dive deep in order to feel her way forward.

All throughout these three books, Smita is deeply connected to her own on board 'Guru', and is always seeking a deeper meaning to her life and existence. While a serious, and at times heart-wrenching book, it also has a wonderful thread of humour woven through. The author has been courageously honest in her accounting, which leaves the reader with a strong connection not only to the story but to this amazing woman too. The character building and scene setting are excellently written, and draw the reader right into the pages, where they walk over the hot coals right along with the author, and feel her tribulations and joys in a personal way. The examples she gives of her life experiences, and the teaching she receives, are clear and easy to understand, and will provide help and guidance to seekers the world over. Here is an enjoyable and informative journal of how a person can move from a life full of struggles to find fulfilment and happiness."

Harmony Kent - Author of 'Elemental Earth' and 'The Glade'

"Smita has done a wonderful job of telling the universal story of each of our heroic journey home to our true Selves. Across continents and lifetimes, she encourages us to trust our inner voice, so we can heal, find more peace and happiness, and to show up as who we truly are."

Nick Williams - Author of 'The Work We Were Born to Do' and 'Pivotal Moments'

Amazon Reviews
for
Karma & Diamonds - Book 1, 'Moon Child'

"Dramatic, moving, inspirational and enlightening - I really enjoyed it."

"Most amazing read ... pulls at your heartstrings, very well written and moves fast. One of my favourites now..."

"Written with an intimacy that takes you into the story, once you start reading you cannot stop, eloquent, colourful and intense ..."

"The dramatic beginning of the book captured my attention and immediately hooked me into the story. I resonated with the innocent and pure voice of the little girl, and her relationship with her Motima, as it reminded me of the one that I have with my own grandchildren."

"This book has made me realise that, while we all have a precious inner Self, we let life get in the way and lose that sense of Self. The author's journey reminds you to question your own decisions, your path and inspires you make brave choices that lead you to be true to that Self."

"The last chapters on meditation were enlightening as I am trying them out. It was also frightening to feel how powerful it can be to find one's Self and try things that you thought were impossible."

"The book ends on a cliffhanger and leaves me wanting to know what happens next, as she sets off for India. I look forward to Book 2."

"This book is one that you can read again and again and get something new every time. The quotes in italics are inspirational and enlightening. I really enjoyed *Karma & Diamonds - Book 1* and will be recommending it to my friends."

"I was captivated by this remarkable story of this spiritual journey. At times I felt it was me and my parallel path."

"Interesting for someone like me who finds it difficult to find the time to read ... with a book like this I found myself making time as it was just riveting."

"I have finished reading *Karma & Diamonds - Moon Child: Book 1* and what an adventure! I loved reading this as it led me to look at my own life's unanswered questions. I can't help but notice some of the similarities in the author's quest in which she has touched on which resonates with me and my life."

"There have been so many a-haa moments in Smita's story which I can so resemble and relate to. I'm amazed and shocked both at the same time ... I feel like I have just read my own story."

"A reflection of my life is staring me right in the face! I think this book has come at the right time for me and I thank you, Smita, for writing it. I will now look forward to reading your second book which I am sure will be as gripping as your first."

"This is a brave, sensitive, heartfelt account of the early life struggle of a gifted spiritual woman. The author gives a wonderful readable account of her journey from a troubled childhood in India to becoming a successful confident woman in the UK. For those who reflect on the mysteries of life and spirituality, this book is a must-read."

"Smita Joshi is a wonderful writer. This book is full of insights and is a great and moving read which identifies how life experiences are of lasting consequence. I could not put it down and cannot wait to read book 2."

"One's journey to self-awareness, acceptance and healing can be traumatic for many of us, with some never reaching the end of the journey. I enjoyed this book tremendously because it struck a chord in me: bitterness about personal traumas can be overcome through self-knowledge and a belief in our inner-voice. The story is compelling and gripping – a must for anyone who is interested in how people can overcome traumas in a world of shifting personal and cultural values."

"As soon as I picked up *Karma & Diamonds*, I was hooked - I couldn't put it down. For me, an English girl who had grown up in peace and stability in London, Smita's book was a real eye-opener to how it was to have a childhood in India. I wouldn't want to spoil the 'story' of the book but suffice to say I felt moved to tears, laughter and intrigue in equal measure. I would definitely recommend the book and am looking forward to the next two!"

"Was wrapped up in this book, which explored the powerful dynamics that challenged Smita as she aspired to search for her truth. An interesting read which exposes insightful philosophical messages. Looking forward to reading *Book 2 - Web of Karma*."

"Through her incredible story, Smita raises and answers many profound questions about life, its purpose, how to live it ... What's more, she does that in a very 'real' rather than esoteric or theoretical way, citing her own personal experiences in a very honest and authentic manner. I found the book fast-paced, gripping and very relevant to my life. As a reader, I felt profoundly related to, and an active part of Smita's journey, even stopping to ask the same questions about my life that she asks about hers. Can't wait to read the next part ..."

An awe-inspiring journey of Self-discovery
across continents and lifetimes

Karma
&
Diamonds

Book 2 - WEB OF KARMA

Smita Joshi

Published by
Filament Publishing Ltd
16, Croydon Road, Waddon, Croydon,
Surrey, CR0 4PA, United Kingdom
Telephone +44 (0)20 8688 2598
Fax +44 (0)20 7183 7186
info@filamentpublishing.com
www.filamentpublishing.com

ISBN 978-1-910819-20-3

Printed by 4edge Ltd

For my Dad

&

With the deepest love and gratitude to
my beloved
Mum,
Grandmother
and
Mahadevi, the Mother Eternal

Acknowledgements

I have so many people to acknowledge for their love and encouragement in bringing about my project and I am grateful to each one of them.

It has been nothing short of a blessing and good fortune to come across someone with the stature of Chris Griscom. A pioneer, she has brought to us to new levels of understanding of how time, emotional imprints, karma and reincarnation interweave to impact the quality of our daily existence; her work ventures into new frontiers in how we can set ourselves permanently free from their hold over us. Chris' work and teachings have helped me to understand my emotional and spiritual world in ways that have altered the direction of my life.

My heartfelt gratitude to Chris for providing a generous and insightful Foreword for this book.

For my friend Ushma Tank, loving appreciation for introducing me to Landmark Education.

I have great love and respect for the work of Landmark Education and the massive difference that it has made in my life, and to the world in general. A special thank you to the phenomenal leaders at Landmark Education - David Ure, Johnny Tenn, Nick Andrews,

Jonathan Stanley, among others - for the mind-blowing inspiration that they've been in my transformation.

Love and gratitude to my family and friends in Rajkot and Ahmedabad for their kindness and generosity in facilitating parts of my journey that inspired some of the writing in this book.

I offer my heartfelt gratitude to:

Tom Evans, for being an inspirational and exceptional mentor.

Harmony Kent, for excellent editing of the three books.

Pieter Weltevrede, the artist extraordinaire, for allowing me to share his divinely inspired art on my book covers and website (www.karma-and-diamonds.com).

Robert Thé, for his skilful insights with the early version of the book as well as for his practical encouragement throughout.

Arpit Kaushik, whose earliest feedback encouraged me to keep going.

Lucie Feighan, for her priceless insight and friendship over the years.

Arvind Devalia, for being an awesome stand for my completing this book.

Mark Booth, for helping me to shape this book into its current form.

A big thank you to the exceptionally talented Robert Sturman for the cover photo of Book 2, *Web of Karma*.

My Love Man, Edwin, whose patient commitment and unwavering devotion pulled me through my darkest moments of writing, when I would rather have given up. I love and adore you - more than I could put into words in any trilogy.

Table of Contents

Foreword by Chris Griscom

Dear Soul Friends,

It is an honor to speak for Smita Joshi's wonderful trilogy, *Karma & Diamonds*. I have never read an autobiography so compelling as this one: beautifully written, emotionally gripping and awe-inspiring.

Aside from exquisite story telling, the book illuminates the power and truth of multi-incarnations in our lives in such a way as to bring us to new octaves of understanding who we are from a spiritual, cosmic perspective. To be transported into Smita's present and past lives with such a sense of clarity, opens us to the vista of how conscious awareness can completely change our possibilities.

Smita brings us a voice of consciousness, inviting us on a journey that transcends customs and cultures; and delivers us directly into the presence of our own essence that we did not know how to access, or even that it truly exists. This is a gift far beyond the simple telling of a story. Aspects of her journey may trigger points of emotional association, but the real treasure is the myriad of beautiful spiritual concepts the stories bring to us.

The lifetimes that Smita accessed and presented within the trilogy echo to each and all of us the very themes we, ourselves, need to elucidate in this lifetime in order to set ourselves free from the clutches of karma. Themes of unrequited love, punishment for talents, and the contracts and vows we make stifle our present incarnation. It is only the deep unconscious current of knowing that pushes us through karmic realities to find the end—and eternally, the new beginning.

These unfolding stories take us through wider and wider arcs of repetitious patterns that bind us from lifetime to lifetime. The gift of incarnational exploration helps us to discover that we absolutely do carry our experiences and predilections with us through many incarnations; and that once we touch them with our consciousness, we can release them or use their essence energies to quicken the evolution of our Soul.

A perfect example of this karmic theme transference is Smita's incarnational lifetime when she and her mother were hanged by the neck for their intuitive and healing capacities. First of all, I feel that this is a universal theme for all humans; and therefore, a brilliant example of what Smita is presenting in her trilogy. We are terrified of our own intuition and any attributes that are above or beyond explanation. Part of our fear is that at least 90 percent of us have been killed for these "paranormal" qualities in our own "past lives." According to historical records, over six million people were tortured and burned at the stake during the Middle Ages because of supposed witchcraft relating to healing or being associated to unexplainable phenomenon. These terrible experiences are deeply encoded within us, and still influence the way we interact today.

Smita carried into this current lifetime her sense of abandonment and blame of her mother, and essentially replayed the hanging theme in an amplified manner. The experience of being choked by her mother as a child, poignantly revisits the karma set in motion by that earlier incarnation—while replacing the angry mob with her mother.

As she comes to realize how her present resentment and guilt covers the deepest love for her mother, we see another example of the Emotional Body's defense mechanisms. We cover our feelings of helplessness, vulnerability and hurt with anger and justification, and rarely glimpse the underlying energy of love. The resolution of this karmic entrapment which Smita experienced, teaches us a great deal about the power of consciousness and the freedom to re-invent ourselves. For me, one powerful measure pertaining to any source of new information is the sudden rush of energy in the form of "goose-bumps" arising on my skin when something is presented, and my inner-knowing confirms its relevance. This physical phenomenon signals to me that something true and real is being illuminated. It often occurs when I have a pre-cognition or flash of a possible event, as well as when I listen to someone telling a story about their life. So it has been in this fantastic trilogy, in which at various points I have experienced that powerful resonance with Smita's words.

Smita opens us to the power of our own Higher Self, the "Inner Diamond," and thus transforms herself as a storyteller, into a magnificent teacher—one who can unabashedly introduce spiritual truths such as the phenomenon of reincarnation, and show us its relevance in our business, social and personal lives. We are blessed to learn all this from Smita's engaging wit, clarity, and sense of profound human wisdom.

With great respect and love,

Chris Griscom
Author of *Ecstasy is a New Frequency, Time Is an illusion* and leading authority on reincarnation

Author's Introduction

This is the book that I wish someone had written for me when I really needed it. The *Karma & Diamonds* trilogy is a compelling and uplifting set of stories about dealing with modern life, stories you want to pick up and be touched and inspired by again and again.

It's a handbook for living the contemporary life while being connected to something deeper within.

The ancient sages of India have described *Atman*, the higher Self, in great detail in the sacred texts. However, accessing it and connecting to it is a whole other matter. Why is it important? How can you access it? How does it look and feel? What difference will it make to be more aware of its presence? What difference will being connected to it make in your life? How can it improve the quality of your everyday life?

I have written this trilogy for those of you who, like me, are seeking to harness your inner radiance and power—whether it be for being more peaceful, feeling more alive and vibrant, or living the best life you possibly dare to.

"There is a false belief that the opposite of suffering is happiness.

Real happiness is a natural consequence of something else: like a rose in bloom exudes its sweet scent, real happiness is an inevitable expression of being rooted in the rich soil of 'Atman', the inner Self."

1

The Big Unknown

As I flew to India, I had time—too much time—to reflect on what I had done. I had thrown myself into the big unknown, which had turned my mind into a loft where crazed squirrels on crack ran amok. This wasn't helped by the reaction of my cousin Avinash, in Ahmedabad airport. His so-called welcome merely put my worst fears on loudspeaker.

"What on earth made you throw away your amazing job at the drop of a hat? And that super BMW with it? Have you gone completely mad? Will you ever find another job like that one again? What could be so important that you'd just chuck away everything you've worked so hard for? What is it exactly that you're here to do, anyway?" Avinash wiped the beads of perspiration from his forehead with his sweat-soaked handkerchief. "And what made you want to come in this sweltering season, Smita? May is the worst month to visit Ahmedabad."

He seemed genuinely panicked about what I had done. Like so many people I knew, he needed be in control of his life. He needed certainty to feel good about himself. Only then could he begin to think about being happy.

I had fond memories of us growing up together until I left India at the age of ten, and I'd made a point of visiting Avinash and his family whenever I was in the country.

"I've missed you *so* much and I couldn't wait to see you again!" I said, cheekily, grinning as I gave him a bear hug.

After all, how on earth was I going to explain to my materially focused, Gujarati family that I had taken a sabbatical from my work so that I could come to India to 'find' myself? As Avinash's reaction betrayed, they would see it only as a foolish folly or conclude that I must be in terrible trouble with my life. After all, who throws away the comfort of a good material life for the austerity of a whimsical, so-called Self-discovery?

I had landed at Ahmedabad Airport in the excruciating 45°C heat of the Gujarati summer. Armed with only a copy of the *Autobiography of a Yogi* by Paramhansa Yogananda, about which my grandfather Motabhai had raved since I was a child. And, also *Himalayan Masters* by Swami Rama, a book that jumped out at me among piles and piles of similar books in the famed Watkins bookshop in London's Covent Garden. All I knew was that I had come in search of 'something more' and hoped for inspiration in these books. If anyone knew about this 'something more', it would be these quintessential mystical seekers, revered for their success in having discovered what 'it' was.

Avinash was half-soaked with sweat in the excruciating heat, as was everyone else around us. He had come to pick me up from the airport, and I couldn't wait to get out of the unforgiving midday sun and into his car. As we crossed the road outside and walked towards the car park, hopscotching through the chaotic traffic of Jeeps, old models of Ambassador and Fiat cars, clapped-out black and yellow motor rickshaws hooting the sirens of their horns, Vespa mopeds and fancy Hero Honda motorbikes, I prayed that my cousin had a car with air conditioning that was in good working order. Such things could not be taken for granted in the chaos of India.

"Your car's a Jeep," I remarked, climbing in.

"No! It's not cheap! It's a very expensive car!" He did not look happy.

"I said, Jeep, *buddhu*, not cheap." I laughed. As his cousin, I considered it my privilege to call him *buddhu* (silly fool). He laughed, embarrassed for being defensive.

"Don't get me wrong, it's always great to see you, but we won't be able to go travelling anywhere in this sweltering sauna of a land," he said.

While he complained about the heat, I noticed that he wore thick, light blue denim jeans, a checked blue and white flannel shirt, and black lace-up shoes and socks. This wasn't untypical in India, and I could never fathom why anyone would want to wear such heavy clothing in such temperatures. Avinash's sister had once told me, when I'd asked about it, that they were so used to it, they didn't even think about it.

"Don't worry," I laughed, looking at Avinash. "I've brought you some lovely summer clothes from London that you'll be able to change into for our travels in this fabulous air-conditioned Jeep of yours."

"Oh no. What have you got in mind this time? Where are you going to drag me to now? I still remember how much trouble we got ourselves into with one of your mad escapades all the way to the interior of the lion-infested Gir Forest!" he said, and pulled his face into an expression of pretend despair at the thought of my dragging him on another adventure. Though I felt certain he secretly looked forward to the prospect.

Of course, I didn't tell him I was clueless as to what I was going to do while in India, as he was already alarmed enough that I had resigned from a perfectly good, well-paid job and the state-of-the-art BMW that came with it.

Now I had taken this leap of faith, my Inner Diamond would surely lead me to my next steps. My training in 'being present' had begun, and all I had to do was enjoy going from one moment to the next, keep vigilantly listening to my intuition, and watch out for synchronicities to arise. But for this to happen, I had to let go of worrying about the unknowns and trying to force outcomes to create certainty.

No, this was a lesson in flowing with uncertainty.

That evening, old friends of my mum came to visit my aunt at Avinash's family's house, where I would be staying for a few days. Back in the day, my mum and Kajalben had been roommates at Gujarat University. Kajalben studied Engineering while my mum followed in her father's footsteps in reading Law.

"Goodness! We had no idea you were in town. What a wonderful surprise." A delighted Kajalben hugged me. "The last time we saw you was when? Almost ten years ago?"

"Exactly. I had just turned eighteen then. That was my first trip back to India after going to London." I remembered how well I'd clicked with Kajalben, her husband Rohitbhai, and her two young sons, Arya and Ayush.

"So what's the plan, Smita, for your stay in India?" Rohitbhai asked.

I laughed. "Well, I don't have one as yet. I'd like to learn something about our spiritual culture, you know—get a better understanding of our ancient texts, maybe meet some knowledgeable *gurus* that we're always hearing about in the West. The thing I'd love to do most is use the time to meditate somewhere quiet. To be honest, I really don't know where to go for any of this."

I felt a bit nervous at the risk of sounding like a flake to these hard-headed business folk.

"Well, we have a house that's just lying empty in Rajkot. It's fully furnished and all, but we haven't stayed there in ages. Why don't you stay there for a while? We can get someone to come and clean the place regularly and maybe even cook for you," Kajalben said, enthusiastically.

"No kidding! That's very generous of you. But I don't want to put you to any trouble." I was surprised and delighted, but mostly humbled, by their generosity.

Before I had a chance to think about it, Rohitbhai added, "That's a great idea, Kajal. We could introduce Smita to our dear friend, Swami Jitatmananda, at the Ramakrishna Ashram. He's very knowledgeable in the *shastras* (ancient texts). I'm sure you'll learn a lot from him, Smita. He used to be a nuclear physicist, you know, before he decided to become a monk. A wonderful man!" His accent sounded posh but also sweet, with its Indian-English nuances. Rohitbhai's mannerisms were more English than an Englishman of the Raj period. He could have stepped right off the pages of a Rudyard Kipling novel.

"In fact, Kajal, why don't we drive Smita to Rajkot, since we have to go there anyway to sort things out at the factory." They had a thriving business, which he had started from nothing, of manufacturing parts for cars.

"Yes, of course." Kajalben said. "That's a great idea. Why not use our Rajkot house as the base from which to undertake your study and meditation? And why don't we take you to meet Swami Shivananda, too? He was an eye surgeon before he chose to become a monk. He now runs a hospital specialising in eye disorders and travels all over India with a team of specialists, conducting eye operations for free for those who can't afford to pay. He's pretty extraordinary too!"

I wondered if my higher Self had already been in touch with the higher Selves of these people and planned my every step before I had even stepped a foot on Indian soil. Some people might have diminished such turn of events as pure coincidence, but to me they were awe-inspiring. Was I beginning to flow with 'higher time?' Was this what being in the right place at the right time felt like: easy, effortless and joyful—just like I had read in that book that Gina had given to me that evening in Covent Garden?

Before I knew it, in true Indian fashion, even before my first night's sleep in India, my fate had been decided for me in the most unexpected and wonderful way. How astonishing was the sheer synchronicity of this meeting, and the enthusiastic generosity of these people. Then again, this was India and this was the kindness of the Indian spirit in action. This, in India, was how people honoured their relationships with each other.

It struck me too, how exceptional it was that both the monks that our friends had mentioned were men of worldly knowledge as well as the spiritual. And moreover, it seemed that they were putting both to good use in service of others.

Had not my Inner Diamond counselled me to integrate the material world with the spiritual? Were these *swamis*, monks of a high order, to be my teachers in this near impossible task? Would one of them perhaps initiate me into my mystical development?

"The secret
is that
there is nowhere to get to.
You are already there.
'Sat Chit Ananda'
awakened, conscious, blissful being:
that is your true nature."

2

Comfort Zone

Once I'd settled into the Maliks' house in Rajkot, I attended discourses with Swami Jnananada and Swami Shivananda. One had his *ashram* in the chaotic centre of Rajkot, while the other was in a small village a few miles outside of town. I picked their brains about their beliefs, the differences between the various *gurus'* lineages, and philosophy.

"Why don't you join us on the eye camp trip that we are going on next week, Smita?" Swami Shivananda said. "There's a team of us going. It'll be an opportunity to see how we do *seva* (service) in India."

Swami Shivananda, looking the part in his orange monk's garb and a forehead adorned with three stripes of holy ash or *vibhuti*, also known as *bhasma*, had devoted his life to serving others. By profession, he had been an eye surgeon and had set up a hospital that specialised in eye-related issues. Now, as a monk, he took a team of volunteer eye surgeons every year to provide free eye operations at medical camps for poor people across India. In the West, such philanthropy would be much publicised but in India, these types of social projects were not uncommon and went on in relative anonymity. Being of service to others was considered one's duty and a privilege.

"Gosh! Really? Where will you be going?" I asked, thrown with surprise. After all, I had only met this orange-garbed *guru* for the first time a couple of weeks ago.

"We'll go to Haridwar, Rishikesh, and some villages along the Himalayan foothills. We'll be gone for about a month," he replied.

"Sounds interesting," I said thoughtfully, but holding back from committing. "Where will you be staying?"

"In *ashrams*, guest lodges, and anywhere that can house us," he replied with an air of detachment. "Just be prepared to sleep on floors and any spaces where you can lay down your head."

My mind flooded with images of unnamed creepy insects crawling around in the dark of communal dormitories with tatty, old, stained, smelly duvets made with coarse cotton wool farmed in local fields, and rural hole-in-the ground outdoor toilets. I shuddered at the thought of *roti* breads and chapattis made by hands with questionable hygiene and yoghurt *lassi* drinks made with water drawn from the wells that were home to who-knows-what kind of beastly bacteria. As soon as I noticed my thoughts, I felt ashamed at my own snobbery.

While the idea of travelling with the *guru* and his entourage serving the poor people of India was exotic for a girl largely accustomed to living in London, I surprised myself with this immediate resistance at the prospect of giving up my creature comforts. I was also not convinced that I would be able to endure the austerities involved, even for just a month. I realised just how attached I was to my relatively pampered life in London: my centrally-heated home with fresh, sanitised hot water showers, clean, cold refrigerated water straight from the tap, flushable toilets that were easy to keep squeaky clean; soft cushy pillows, Egyptian cotton bedsheets with matching covers for soft, comfy duvets that compelled you to have cosy lie-ins on Sunday mornings.

"Hmmm ... I see," I said, hesitant.

The Swamiji, tickled pink at what must have looked like horror in my facial expression, laughed out loud. "You want to know if you can stay in a five-star hotel and still come with us, isn't it? Hahaha!" He was really enjoying the irony. Meanwhile, I'd gone red with embarrassment at being so transparent, and he was right—that's exactly what I was thinking. The notion of soul searching in the comfort of my warm well-furnished flat with all the latest modern conveniences seemed so appealing but, now that I was here, in the inlands of India, the reality was all too real.

Not wishing to appear nefarious, I set about trying to make a case for slithering out of going on this trip. "Swamiji, what use will I be to you? Your volunteers are all surgeons, pharmacists, and qualified nurses. I'll only get in their way!"

"Hahaha! Is that so?" He laughed loudly again.

His jovial and open manner reminded me of my beloved grandfather, Motabhai, who lived just a few hundred miles away. Just as Motabhai came to mind, I suddenly had another reason to decline. He would have a coronary when I told him that I was off gallivanting all across India with some monk. Motabhai would surely not approve. He would probably say that he and my parents had not educated me just so I could give up life in the world. Would he understand this business about integrating the material world with the spiritual?

I was sure the hard-hitting lawyer in him would dismiss my soul searching, saying something dismissive like, "You are either a monk or a householder. The rest is cloud cuckoo land!" Only losers, according to him, became monks.

The *guru* continued to read me. My eyelashes fluttered rapidly like a bat's wings in full flight, a dead giveaway that I was distracted by my internal dialogue.

"Smita, you're too attached to your creature comforts and your idea of how life should look. This is the perfect opportunity in learning to let go. All those things that define you, let them go, just for a few days, and see what opens for you—the posh hotels you stay in, the upscale places you eat at, the clothes you wear. Come with us and learn about who you are without all those things that you think are who you are." Swami Shivananda had a cheeky twinkle in his eye, challenging me. Perhaps he knew more about why my Inner Diamond had brought me here than I did.

"But what will I do there?" I said, almost whining, like a petulant child objecting to her punishment.

"*Nimmittamatram bhava*," the monk Swami replied in a gentle, kind tone, quoting from the *Bhagavad Gita*. "Be a mere instrument." I couldn't help being impressed when I heard people of the renunciate's cloth reel off quotes, and even entire passages, in Sanskrit from sacred texts, of which there were thousands. He smiled at me, his eyes twinkling. "You have come to me to learn what it is to serve, forget yourself, and to remember your Self."

The elegance of sophisticated Sanskrit made even having a wash in a cold clay pond sound like bathing in a crystalline lake. Frankly, learning to do *seva*, to serve, sounded to me about as exciting as digging ditches in the Arabian Desert. However, I knew full well that my Inner Diamond had not brought me all the way to the inlands of India in such a dramatic fashion so that I could luxuriate mindlessly in five-star hotels.

"When do we leave?" I asked, sighing, resigned to my fate.

Swamiji smiled. I had hit upon the first hurdle of self-discovery that stops many a so-called seeker: sacrificing comfort. I was attached to my creature comforts, to being comfortable in my emotional and mental boundaries, and generally being in my comfort zone. Would I survive the journey? Or would I hop on the first train back to Rajkot?

Was this what self-discovery looked like? The irony was that how I saw myself was entirely different. It was already a revelation to discover just how attached I was to being *comfortable*.

"The soul inhabits human forms
so that it can undertake
'karma' or actions
that will lead to
its liberation from 'samskaras',
the imprints of desires and trauma
that have accumulated
on the mind, the senses,
and
the body."

3

Selfless Service

I loved making long journeys on the railways of India. Never sitting in the cold of air-conditioned first class carriages, I would rather take the second class upper bunk so that I would not miss a minute of the beautiful breeze that flowed through the iron-barred open windows. It was tradition, and therefore unthinkable, to travel without bringing cooked food, which tasted all the more delicious because it was consumed as a picnic on an Indian railway, fast shooting through vast open spaces of the Indian countryside. Usually, you would share your packed meals and club them together with whatever others in your group had brought, making mealtimes of long rail journeys communal feasts to be savoured.

Though I was a long way from home, my newly made friends in Rajkot, introduced to me by the kind Malik family, had insisted on packing me a brown paper bag full of picnic food that resembled the meals that Grandma Motima used to make for us. A large pile of slightly crisped, spiced *thepla*, yellow flatbreads shallow fried on a hot iron griddle, accompanied by dry potato curry spiced with turmeric, flavoured to perfection with diced green chillies and small cubes of ginger, tempered in hot sunflower oil with cumin and mustard seeds, green *neem* or curry leaves and salt. I remembered that, as a little girl, whenever we travelled on trains, we would also bring for our picnics on these trains Motima's exquisite spicy pickles of shredded and diced green mangoes, sun-dried in the Gujarati summer sun on the rooftop terrace of our home in Porbandar.

That said, the height of summer, with its intemperate heat, wasn't the best time to make long journeys across India. On the journey on which we had just set off, the cool breeze was horribly amiss and, instead, we were made to suffer hot summer gusts of dusty wind that swirled across the dry deserts through which our Indian rail sped.

Normally, I would find the long, three-day journey from Rajkot to Rishikesh insufferable but, as the train sped across India, time flew in the pleasant and jovial company of the group of volunteers I was travelling with. We played the game of *antakshari*, singing well-known Bollywood songs in Hindi, many whose lyrics I still remembered, as if I had learnt them just yesterday, from those years of growing up in India. It was a fun game where you had to sing a song whose lyrics started with the vowel or consonant on which the previous singer's song had ended, thereby making a continual musical chain of songs that people loved and that made them all too sentimental about memories of their fondly remembered past.

The early morning sing-song of the *chaiwallas*— vendors selling hot, sweet, spiced Indian tea—at train stops woke us up at the crack of dawn. Thousands of gallons of hot masala chai must have been consumed in those early hours, bringing weary night travellers into the life of a new day. The hubbub at the stations in the dawn hours, with the sun busy shedding its light and warmth across the vastness of India, had a special quality to it. Even on the train platforms, a sanctity was granted to the sacredness of dawn where, amidst their morning activity, people went about their business respectfully, bearing in mind the divinity contained in these early hours.

From Haridwar, a private coach took us to Rishikesh. This small town came into Western awareness when the Beatles, in the 1960s, came to stay at the *ashram* of Rishi Mahesh Yogi. The Beatles spent weeks meditating here and wrote some thirty songs during their stay. John Lennon even recorded a song called the *Happy Rishikesh Song*.

Rishikesh, in the Ganges plains, the gateway to the Himalayas, was the starting point of a Hindu pilgrimage called the *Char Dham Yatra*, or the pilgrimage to the four most sacred spots of Gangotri, Jamnotri, Kedarnath, and Badrinath. Every spiritually aspiring Hindu considered himself fortunate to be called to pay a visit to these places. Rishikesh itself was said to be the birthplace of yoga and spirituality—a place where *ashrams*, new and old, gave unconditional refuge to people of any creed, colour, and race.

It was as if time had stood still here in this ancient town. The rickshaws—some painted with curvaceous Bollywood stars with pouty red lips and glossy hair, others simply with splashes of bright colours—weaved in and out between the larger vehicles. Roads heaved with old clunky Fiats, Ambassadors, Marutis, and more modern SUVs, hooting all the way to their destination. Not to mention the brazenly yet delightfully painted lorries, stating the customary 'Horn Please', each with declarations at the top of their windscreens in Hindi for their beloved India. They bullied road users out of their way with loud, sassy sirens. Then there were the rusty buses with missing window panes revealing tired passengers eager to reach home; prided motorbikes expertly manoeuvred; carefree students at home on their mopeds and bicycles; thin, *sari*-clad women walked gracefully along the road, balancing heavy cargoes on their heads; men chewed betel nut and green *paan* leaves, making spittoons of the road with their bitter, red tobacco fixes. The animals had their place too: cows, oblivious to their surroundings, sat peacefully in the most unlikely of places in the middle of the road, snacking on leftovers from the vegetable vendors on the roadside or simply having a rest, and street dogs wandered about, waiting for the night hour to make their howling presence felt.

It seemed that all of life was gathered on this one road of this antiquated town, making a cacophony of sound—the sound of India. Yet, somehow, for me there was comfort in this cacophony, the kind of comfort that you get from knowing that you are home. Whatever opinion you might have about the lack of harmony on Indian roads or chaos on the trains, however much you may wish India to be better organised, to be cleaner, I felt right at home here. My motherland opened its arms in a warm embrace to welcome all who came here. I was home, just as much as in London, despite them being two very different homes.

As we came into Rishikesh town, on the way to our *ashram*, the coach stopped for a few minutes near Lakshman Jhula, the picturesque suspension bridge that, like an irresistible hammock on a hot summer's day, dangled luxuriously over the River Ganga (Ganges). Rajan, Anika, and I walked onto the footbridge, where the only vehicles were bicycles, scooters, and motorbikes. Surprised to be greeted by mischievous monkeys eager to playfully snatch away our food and sunglasses, we stood soaking up the panoramic majesty of the glorious River. She had a life and character all of her own, a sovereignty that one dared not impede. Even from high on up, with the elegant and voluptuous curves of her banks, she impressed with her grand beauty and charismatic presence, drawing you into the net of her seduction, enticing you to fall in love with her the instant you set sight on her. This was the power of Ganga Ma—giver of life.

When we finally arrived at our *ashram* in the Himalayan foothills, half an hour from the centre of the ancient Rishikesh, and far from the chaos of the city, it turned out to be a newly built site with many acres of flowering gardens and carefully manicured grounds. It had room enough for our entire party to stay here— the men in communal dormitories, while women were given rooms to share. I had been paired up with Anika, an eye surgeon from Rajkot. She was at least five to seven years older than me. We had already spent some time in each other's company on the train, and we had clicked well with each other.

Our room was simple but impeccable, with a small bathroom that had just a cold water tap and a plastic bucket to fill for our 'shower', and there was also a separate Indian toilet. The two single wooden beds had traditional tightly woven jute rope to give them a firm base. The mattresses were firm, hard even, made from tightly packed coarse cotton wool, as were the single pillows placed on each bed. The folded white cotton sheet at the base of the bed would suffice for cover during the hot nights, made cooler by a ceiling fan. This was already more than I had expected, and merely the cleanliness of our room was enough to remove my earlier concerns.

Early the next morning at the eye camp, which had already been set up by local volunteers when we arrived at seven o'clock, the job that Swamiji allocated to me was to clean up after the surgeons undertaking cataract operations. I had to clean and prepare the space for the next operation. I was also tasked with looking after the patients by making them comfortable until it was their turn to be operated on as well as afterwards, until they were ready to leave. I ran back and forth from the tea and snacks tent, fetching them cups of sweet, hot chai to soothe their nerves after the operation.

I found myself blown away with inspiration as I watched the surgeons at work. Each operation took just minutes and they executed each one impeccably, despite the makeshift tents in the middle of dusty fields that made for operating theatres. Queues of poor people, some with clothes that were dirty and torn from toiling in the fields, lined up from early morning to night, and still no one was turned away. For them, the opportunity of new sight was nothing short of *kripa*, God's grace. They were offered hot meals, freshly cooked on-site throughout the day by teams of yet more volunteers, and not a penny was taken in return.

As I worked in these camps, amidst these dirt-poor people and in the immensity of selflessness expressed by the doctors and nurses who healed them, my own petty internal conversation died away as I realised only too well what a relatively privileged life I led. Say what you might about the cleanliness, or the lack of it, of the holy River Ganges, I felt its sacredness permeate me simply by stepping foot in its icy coldness, washing away the hardness and sadness that still pained my heart from my past. Could it be that the magic of the nearby Himalayas, from where these cold, crystal waters had been springing for thousands of years, now palpated in my spirit by simply dipping even just a toe in this mystical river?

At the end of the first day of service, we were exhausted both from the ceaseless running around and the heat, and I wanted nothing more than my *ashram* bed to crash into after dinner. But Swami Shivananda had other plans.

"Swamiji has told me to tell you that he wants you to join the *satsang* gathering tonight," Rajan told me. He and I had become friends during my visits to the Swami's *ashram* outside Rajkot. The train journey had served to bond various people in the group, including myself and Rajan.

"What? When?" I said, instantly irritated. "Can't you tell him I'm knackered? I can't be bothered to sit through a long lecture tonight!"

"No. You have to be there. He was quite insistent that you have to attend." Rajan appeared near to panic that I might disobey.

"Why are you so distressed? Goodness! Anyone would think God himself is about to appear," I said, pursing my lips, and making a sour face while slouching my shoulders with resignation.

"No, no! You have be there," Rajan said, more insistently.

"Are you scared of him, Rajan? I'm not." I felt defiant. "Besides, I don't take too well to being commanded to do stuff."

"It's not about being scared. It's about being respectful. In India, we are respectful to our elders and particularly revered monks and the like." Rajan was almost shaking with passion in his speech. I could see that he was sincere while I had somehow forgotten my Indian upbringing. We were taught to be respectful to our elders, especially mother and father figures, never answering back, regardless of whether you agreed or disagreed with them.

He continued to chide me. "And you're mistaken in thinking that way, Smita. He's not commanding you, well, okay, I guess he is when you look at it from the Western culture. But you have to understand that in India, especially when coming from an elder family member or someone of Swamiji's stature, it's a mark of affection and acceptance. In this case, it's a sign that Swamiji's taken you under his wing. Believe me, this doesn't happen often and certainly not so quickly."

"Really?" I paused for a moment as memories came flooding back. "Okay, actually, now that I think of it, Motabhai, my grandfather in Porbandar, talks to me that way. I even get irritated when he does it. Gosh. Have I become that Westernised?" I stretched my tightly closed lips across my jaw, raising my shoulders in shame.

"You know, when a *guru* takes you under his wing, especially someone of Swami Shivananda's calibre, it's considered a *karmic* gift, *purva punya* or a reward from good deeds in your past," Rajan said.

I looked at him, quickly getting off my high Western horse where being 'assertive' was what I valued and where obedience was for doormats. "Wow," I muttered humbly. "What a difference a cultural context makes."

"It sure does. You're very lucky. Some people keep coming for years and never find someone like Swamiji to give them *diksha* (initiation). You must be ready when it happens," he said, as he looked at me admiringly and then teased me with asperity. "I wouldn't want you to miss such an amazing opportunity because you didn't 'get' it or because you were more concerned about asserting yourself and not being a pushover or something." He sobered and gave me a serious look. "Be there in half an hour, in the *ashram's* main hall."

I saluted sarcastically. "Yes, Sir!"

"You're so funny!" Rajan laughed. "Oh, before I forget, we're going to do a firewalk tomorrow evening, after dinner, also followed by a *satsang* gathering and afterwards, Swamiji will be giving a very special talk. You mustn't miss that."

"A firewalk? Wow. Of course I won't miss that. I'm a fire junkie, don't you know? I've done quite a few firewalks. Did one just a month ago in London," I said proudly. And it was true, I loved walking on glowing hot coals. It made me feel just as alive as the red-hot coals. "I didn't know they did firewalks in India, too."

"All you foreigners! You're so full of yourselves. You think that you know it all and invented everything, don't you?" Rajan teased abrasively in Indian-English, though somewhat meaning it. "Did you know that the very first known reference to firewalking dates back to 1200BC in India? Our *yogis* and *rishis* have been walking on glowing, red-hot coals for thousands of years." I could see Rajan's pride in our country and its heritage, something I could do with learning from him.

"Really? I can well imagine," I said, smiling. I noticed that I liked Rajan. He was smart, fun, and a brilliant doctor.

Rajan left the room shortly afterwards. Anika, just waiting for the chance—almost jumping up in front of me and grinning cheekily—bobbed her head like a classical Indian dancer and said, "I think someone's got a crush on you!"

"What? Who? What are you talking about?" I said, embarrassed.

She teased. "You know who." I was used to working mostly with men in my career and so I didn't think twice about getting on well with guys.

"Don't be silly. Where I come from, it's normal to laugh and joke with guys you work with or you're on some project with. Besides, his family are friends of our old friends, the Maliks', so there's nothing unusual about being friendly with each other, is there now?"

"Maybe where you come from. Not in India." She laughed.

"Really? We're in the late twentieth century, not the middle ages."

"Well, maybe, but here, girls are still girls and boys are boys, and things are still not as free as you might like to believe," Anika said.

"That old cultural chestnut again." Hmmm ... the guy had a crush on me ... how did I not see that? Was I that naïve? I wondered how many other times I had inadvertently transgressed cultural boundaries and offended people, while going about my business in blissful ignorance.

The thought made my head spin. Overcome with exhaustion, I fell asleep—only to startle awake when I heard, "Wake up, Swamiji's calling you!" Anika said anxiously. "Hurry up! He noticed you weren't there and told me to come and get you."

"Oh, God! I fell asleep. I'm exhausted. Why couldn't Swamiji have waited until tomorrow to start these gatherings?" I said, exasperated, as I shot up from the bed and grabbed my long yellow *dupatta*, the Indian scarf that matched my light cotton Indian dress.

4

Shine

We ran to the main hall and slinked into a small space in the back corner of the otherwise packed and cosily lit hall. I was surprised to see at least a couple of hundred people sitting cross-legged, or on their shins and heels, on the somewhat creaky wooden floor. I had no idea that Swamiji would be so popular. Two *ghee* lamps flickered peacefully in the front of an elegantly carved statue of Lord Ganesh and an oversized golden frame with a painting of Lord Shiva dancing with his beloved Goddess Parvati in these very foothills of Himalaya. Overhead, the whirring fans wafted the fragrant frangipani incense even into the far corner of the room where Anika and I had wedged ourselves a seat on the floor.

Swamiji was already in full swing, looking relaxed and at home sitting on the floor at the front of the room. I marvelled at the fact that he could sit cross-legged on the wooden floor for hours without discomfort, something that I, less than half his age, could not do for even just a few minutes. He beamed with energy as he looked around to see who was present. Did he get much sleep? What sort of food did he eat? Was it different to what we had? How come I was exhausted, being at least thirty-five years younger than him, and he was still bouncing off the walls even after a three-day journey on Indian Railways? What was his secret? Whatever it was, I wanted some of it.

"'In the innermost golden sheath there is *Brahman* (ultimate reality) without stains and without parts, that is pure, that is the light of lights. That is what the knowers of the *Atma* know,' so it says in the *Mundaka Upanishad* 2.2.9." Swami Shivananda shared with us his deep knowledge of the epic Vedic texts.

"You are a diamond, metaphysically speaking. It is your inherent nature to shine. You are a diamond and it is your nature to sparkle. You will know *Brahman* through its microcosm, which is called *Atman*. It looks like a diamond, dwelling just to the right side of your physical heart. There, the macrocosm filters through the prism of this metaphorical 'diamond' and refracts its light into your being. Giving you life, granting you knowledge, making its wisdom available. Each and every person, each and every one of you has this diamond and it is who you are. You are of this light. Who you are, as your essential self, dwells eternally in this light. A scorpion's nature is to sting. A dog's nature is to bark. A lion's nature is to roar. What is your nature? Your nature is to shine." The orange-robed Swami Shivananda had captured the attention of the seekers, both Indian and foreigners.

"*Taittiritopanishad* 3.6 illumines us thus, '*Anandaddhyeva khalvimani bhutani jayate, Anandena jatani jivanti, Anandam prayantyabhisamvisanti.*' From the transcendental ecstasy, we came into existence. In ecstasy we grow and play our respective roles. At the end of our journey's close, we enter into the supreme ecstasy." Swami Shivananda's knowledge of the ancient texts impressed and humbled me, and hearing perfectly pronounced Sanskrit verses was beautiful from a scholar of Swamiji's calibre.

The idea of coming from 'transcendental ecstasy' and of metaphysically being a sparkling diamond gave me goose pimples. It brought a new, more purposeful context to being a sales executive of a technology company.

"So, how many of you can say that you know yourself that way?" he asked his attentive audience.

"The truth is, you don't. Because you relate to yourself in a very limited way, as someone's son or daughter, the mother or father, the employer or employee, the doer, the thinker. In other words, you only know yourself through your superficial outer layer.

You know yourself only as your identity, your ego. Even then, how many of you can, hand on heart, say that you know the design or the functioning of the ego?"

He paused as he posed the rhetorical question, scouring the lost yet enquiring faces in front of him.

"Your identity appears to be real. It appears to be solid. But it is not. It's merely a flimsy tin wall, the kind you will see separating one hut from the next in the slums that line the railway tracks all up and down India."

As he spoke, the Swamiji became more radiant, as if he was transmitting more than just words.

"Blow away the thin layers of the ego and you'll see that there is a sparkling diamond at your core. This is you. This is who you are!" he said, dripping with power and delight. He seemed so sure.

Oh my God! He was talking about the Inner Diamond. My Inner Diamond. So I hadn't been making it up after all. Other people must be able to feel its presence too. Swamiji had experienced it as well. I felt ecstatic as the realisation dawned on me, now that I had woken up and finally arrived, free of resistance, into the room. I wanted to shout out that I had seen and felt this Diamond within me. That it had connected with me many times. But instead I sat motionless, speechless, now energised and alive, and brought my attention back to Swamiji's words.

"'That *Brahman* (pure consciousness) shines forth, vast, divine, inconceivable, subtler than the subtle. It is far beyond what is far, and yet near here, and seen fixed in the cave of the heart by the wise,' so goes the *Mundaka Upanishad*, 3.1.7." Swamiji paused as his audience soaked up his rich words, spoken first in Sanskrit and then English.

"So, why don't we know ourselves that way?" A foreigner in the audience, with a Dutch accent, shouted out irreverently, much to the annoyance of some of the local Indians who understood the protocol of being polite and graciously respectful in the presence of a holy man of higher knowledge.

After all, knowledge was the tool by which the *guru* freed us of earthly bondage, by dispelling the darkness of ignorance and so allowing the light of knowledge to shine through his presence. Knowledge was light in a world of darkness cast by ignorance. That rare being who sacrificed their life to walking the fire of higher awareness, and being willing to give their life sharing it with others, was indeed exceptional. They, therefore, deserved to be treated with respect.

"That is indeed the million dollar question." Swamiji smiled kindly, unruffled by the interruption. "There are several reasons. One of the most immediate ones is that, with the pressures of modern-day life, it's all too easy to lose touch with our true nature. In the stresses and struggle brought about by the rush of having to have everything immediately, our 'now, now, now' culture, we lose awareness of the lustre that is at our core and we feel disconnected from the sense of vitality, clarity, and strength that resides there. As a result, life becomes a mundane affair and the way we feel about ourselves is far from vibrant."

A vibrancy certainly exuded from Swamiji's eyes, and I couldn't help but notice. His face was aglow, as if an invisible light penetrated his golden Indian skin, giving it an aura of translucence. Was this the light he referred to?

5

Suffering is Only Optional

The Swamiji spoke again, continuing his answer to the rude Dutchman's question.

"Then there is the second reason. This one is much more of a sticky issue. This is a notion that is deeply embedded in our psyche that 'suffering' is somehow normal in life. That suffering is an inevitable part of life—" his flow was again interrupted.

"But it is!" This time, a loud, angry objection came from the back of the room in an American accent. It was an unkempt man, sitting just in front of me and Anika, with blond tresses to his shoulders, donning a lime-green T-shirt with a large, colourful print of Goddess Lakshmi on his back, only instead of the usual four arms, she had eight. "You can't be happy all the time, can you? And when you're not happy, you're suffering. So suffering *is* normal, whether you like it or not, whether you accept it or not."

Not disturbed by another uninvited interruption, Swamiji, as if playfully catching a ball that had just been lobbed at him in a game of cricket, turned to address the blond man directly. "Ah, you see, you are even suffering from the very belief that suffering is normal." Swamiji laughed lightly after he'd addressed the man across the room.

"What's your name, young man?" Swamiji asked, with softness in his voice.

"Paul."

"Paul, are you suffering, as we speak?" Swamiji asked.

"No. I don't think so." His answer sounded somewhat defensive.

"So, would you say that you are at peace in this very moment?" Swamiji probed, directing the dialogue.

"Possibly. Maybe. No," the blond man said.

"Consider, then, that you are suffering. Do you know why you are suffering?" Swamiji enquired.

"Because it's part of my nature as a human being to suffer. Surely, all life is suffering?"

"Ah! You were clearly not present at the beginning of our meeting. Quite to the contrary, your very nature is light. Does the sun suffer? Your inherent nature is to shine," Swamiji said. "Can you see that the very belief that suffering is normal is causing you to suffer?"

"But you just can't be happy all the time. And certainly not when there are so many people who don't even get enough to eat every day, never mind think about being happy."

"You see, in so many cultures, the notion of suffering as being natural is sacrosanct." Swamiji turned to his audience as he emphasised the pervasive nature of this fundamental belief.

"It is almost blasphemous to suggest otherwise. It actually upsets people to suggest otherwise, and so this notion goes unexamined. It lives on, being passed from generation to generation like it's the truth absolute, thereby limiting or killing off joy and fulfilment that are otherwise possible, even available."

He paused briefly, then continued, "Somewhere along the way, we inherited the notion that suffering is inevitable, and that makes you want to give up before you have started something wonderful. It makes you shut down so that you do not have to feel the pain of sadness and anger that might have accumulated over the years. And when you are joyful and happy, it triggers feelings of guilt because there are countless reminders around us that many others are unhappy."

The force of the truth of Swami Shivananda's words pierced me like a bullet between my eyebrows, waking me up wide. Yes, I too had an unconscious belief somewhere within me that had been shaping my life, stripping me of my multidimensionality and, instead, manifesting me as a cardboard cut-out, so that I could avoid feeling my own suffering. This had shut me down from feeling the intensity of 'negative' things. I was beginning to realise that if I was not open to feeling the darkness lurking within me, then I must also be limiting the more pleasurable emotions and feelings, the lighter aspects of my nature.

"What if the underlying premise that we have to be happy is misleading? What if I were to say to you that you don't have to be happy and you don't have to suffer? What would you say to that?" Swamiji asked Paul.

Of course, Swamiji was right. Somewhere deep within me lay a belief that I was totally asleep to: that in life there would be suffering. But what if Swamiji's suggestion was correct? What if the notion that suffering was a given in life was not The Truth? What then?

As if Swamiji was transmitting some palpable yet subtle force, I felt, one by one, beliefs that limited happiness shatter within me, notions that I had picked up somewhere on my soul's journey and carried with me to this very moment.

Paul answered, "Then I wouldn't know what to think. I'd have no framework from which to think and no compass with which to navigate my feelings and emotions."

Paul's willingness to be honest broke open something that had until now been a barrier for him. Right in front of my eyes, I could see something change in him. His combative demeanour softened and his resistance melted, making him look vulnerable, like a true seeker.

"Don't I have good reason to believe that life is suffering, given the horrendous poverty and insane wars that go on in the world and innocent children being molested? And if suffering wasn't part of our narrative, then what other choice do we have? Pretending to be happy is simply not an option."

The American was clearly intelligent and he seemed to have given these issues of life a lot of thought. He was suffering about suffering.

Swamiji replied, "All of what you say exists. Most of our sorrows come from misunderstanding. We misunderstand the people whom we love, because we have not taken the time and trouble to be in their shoes for five minutes. We don't even understand ourselves, because we are too busy looking outside of ourselves for the solutions and answers to our suffering. Take the time to get to know your own inherent nature, your *svabhava*. Then it becomes easier to understand others."

I realised that when we thought about spiritual knowledge, we looked to the stars and the heavens, as if knowledge resided there. But Swamiji was talking about something much more practical. He meant self knowledge as well as Self knowledge, and referred to understanding who you are in your humanity and who you are as a unique spark of the divinity. The gateway to your light, or Self, was through your dense darkness, your humanity. That was the access to understanding who you were, as your higher Self. The higher and the 'lower' self, the ego and the Inner Diamond, had to work hand in hand.

Swamiji continued, "There is a false belief that the opposite of suffering is happiness and the West spends too much time in the pursuit of happiness, but this is futile. It's like chasing fleeting shooting stars. You cannot pursue something so transient as happiness.

Consider that happiness is a by-product of something else. Instead of pursuing something that is fleeting and restless, what if you instead resolved to connect with that which is permanent and changeless?"

It was some years later when I realised more precisely what Swamiji meant by 'something else'. Real happiness arose quite naturally, organically if you will, as a consequence of this 'something else': like a rose in bloom exudes its sweet scent, real happiness is an inevitable expression of being rooted in the rich soil of *Atman*, the inner Self.

The now less angry Paul sat deep in thought. He looked positively unsettled. Just like me, it seemed that he too had a few of his foundational notions shattered in this powerful transmission coming from this profound holy man.

The energy in the room was high, but the concepts that we were being taught by Swamiji were profound. We needed time to percolate what he had just said to us, both verbally and energetically.

"Let us meditate on the inner light," Swamiji said, bringing this dialogue to a close.

"For those of you who are new to meditation or who find it difficult to meditate, look at the flame flickering from this *ghee* lamp. Observe it with your eyes open until you can visualise or sense it in your third eye. Then close your eyes and merely focus on the light from the flame. Those of you that have been meditating for a while, visualise the flame opening the lotus petals at your crown and let the light of *Atman* to pour into your head and heart."

Everyone closed their eyes and, after a while, the shuffling of seats died down, with only the occasional movement to relieve the discomfort of sitting on the floor.

At the end of the meditation, Anika burst out giggling and nudged me sharply with her elbow. I looked at her, wondering why she was being so childish. As she indicated with her thumb to her left, I also could not contain myself from bursting into cackles. A young red-headed, freckled man, reeking somewhat of musky sweat, greasy hair draping over his shoulders, sat with a thin Italian-looking brunette with matted hair, pearly whites for teeth, and a twinkling nose stud. The man had arrived late and Swamiji's attendants had squeezed him into the last remaining space in the room, next to this brunette.

Earlier, the red-headed man had introduced himself with an American drawl to the girl, who gave him a flash of her toothy whites and they seemed to warm to each other almost immediately. As Swamiji imparted his wisdom, the man, taking advantage of the tight floor seating, nudged even closer to the young brunette. Such was the cosy and intimate atmosphere in the room, it wasn't long before he progressed to putting his right arm around her bare, bronzed shoulders and innocently, or so it appeared, caressing her sleeveless skin. The brunette seemed only too happy to indulge his amorous, quixotic advances. Only now, the two of them moved on to snogging proper, right in sight of our giggling faces, full-frontal kissing with all the trimmings, including hand smooching and groping all over each other's backs.

Anika and I were in hysterics. With disbelief, I looked at Anika and mouthed a shocked "O", and my eyes popped out of my head at this guy's audacity. "Cheeky monkey! No suffering going on there," I laughed. It was hilarious to see these two complete strangers going at each other, frisking, as if telling the rest of us, "Chill out, dude!", in full view of a room packed full of unassuming, sincere spiritual seekers.

One of Swamiji's attendants came up to the amorous couple and, with his hands folded in prayer, tried to get their attention. "Please," he whispered sweetly but clearly embarrassed, bobbing his head side-to-side Indian-style, a timid smile on his face. He signalled that he wanted them to take their snogging outside, but they pretended not to hear him and carried right on frisking each other in a passionate flirtation.

Before long, Swamiji's attention was drawn to these shenanigans and a smile broke onto his face, as he joked, "My friends, the *satsang* on Tantrik Kama Sutra is not till tomorrow!" Everyone burst out laughing. "It is okay. You carry on. It is all *karma!*" His head bobbed with joviality, and Anika and I creased up with laughter.

6

Washing Away Karma

One thing that I absolutely wanted to do while in Rishikesh was to bathe in the River Ganga and experience the riverside sunrise *Ganga Aarti*, the collective singing of *bhajans*—devotional songs and hymns to the Goddess Ganga. An *aarti* ceremony consisted of *ghee* lamps or *diyas* being lit and offered to the Goddess Ganga. Believed to be a 'remover of pain', the *aarti* was said to have the power to heal whoever participated with a devoted heart.

I had been prepared to get up as early as 4.30 a.m. to go to the Triveni Ghat, a confluence of the Ganga, Yamuna, and Saraswati rivers. This was where most people went in Rishikesh to bathe to wash away lifetimes of *karma* and to witness the *Ganga Aarti*. On our arrival at the *ashram*, however, to our amazement and delight, we discovered that the *ashram* had its own private *ghat*, an area of the riverbank with steps that led directly into the River Ganga. As if a private access to this special river was not exceptional enough, it turned out that the *ashram* priest, along with the monks, conducted a daily sunrise *puja* ceremony and *Ganga Aarti*.

As a child, I had heard much about the astonishing powers of the River Ganga, the embodiment of sacredness, so pure that its Himalayan-originated waters have the power to grant *moksha* (ultimate liberation of the soul). Her power was such that, not only did it nourish the lands through which it flowed, but also nourished the body, mind, and soul of all who stepped into her flow. I had heard it said a hundred times that just one dip in the Ganges erased ten lifetimes of negative *karma*, and I wanted some of that.

"I'm willing to give it a go," Anika said, although looking sceptical. "Though I'm not sure that it's sacred anymore, what with all the ashes from all those dead bodies cremated at the *ghats* and God knows what other rubbish that's dumped in there. Let's hope that higher up here, away from the crowds of Rishikesh, we'll get a cleaner part of the river."

Anika echoed my own concerns, but something in me also believed that this river still possessed primordial energy and powers, that it still kept its ancient promise. As far as I was concerned, I was all for connecting with it and receiving whatever gift the River Goddess wanted to grant.

We approached the river, bathed in the soft early morning golden glow from the slowly rising sun after its night slumber. Our *ashram* was several miles outside of Rishikesh, up into the foothills of the Himalayas, and we were fortunate that it had large grounds that backed directly onto a narrower part of the Ganges, giving us almost exclusive access to the otherwise overcrowded and polluted riverbanks that were accessible from within Rishikesh. Apart from me and Anika, there was no one else yet at the riverbank. I wanted to take a dip and offer my prayers into the sacred river, before the priest and monks arrived to conduct the *aarti* ceremony, so that we could change into dry clothes in between the two events.

"I remember the first time I went to the Ganga River. I was just seven or eight years old, when my dad took me with him to Haridwar. He got into the Ganga first, and then asked his friend to throw me in so he could catch me, and then he dunked me into the icy-cold water a few times. I had no idea it would be so cold, so you can imagine how I shrieked and yelled. But I loved it!" I couldn't help smiling at the sweet memory. "That was the first and the last time for me in the River Ganga, until now."

"This will be my first time," Anika said. "I've never been on a pilgrimage or anywhere so close to the Himalayas."

"Well, brace yourself," I said.

At first, I paddled gingerly in the glacial ice water, despite the heat of the Indian summer. With no culture of wearing bathing suits, we stepped in fully clothed in our white cotton Indian *salwar khameez* suits.

Anika walked in me behind me, immediately letting out a shriek or two from the shock of the icy water biting her legs.

Once accustomed to the chilly temperature of the river, its green-blue flow calming and gentle at the riverbank, I found a sandy spot underfoot on which to ground myself and turned east to face the rising sun. With my eyes closed, I imagined that its light, warming open the third eye at my forehead, was sinking deep into every cell of my brain and into the mind beyond, and that the solar rays blossomed open the heart centre and the thousand petals of the lotus that was supposed to reside at my crown, just as Swamiji had said last night. Then, I recited the *Gayatri Mantra*, a solar *mantra*, to invoke and absorb the spiritual energy of the sun, its light synonymous with higher and mystical knowledge. I had no idea of what I was about to experience next, and offered a single flower petal into the river with the repetition of each *mantra*, and a prayer of gratitude for these abundant mystical blessings.

"Your face! You're glowing, Smita!" Anika exclaimed as she turned and walked over to me on the shallow riverbed when she'd had enough of being in deeper water. "What happened to you? You look vibrant."

"Do I? I'm probably just flushed from the rays of the sun." I hesitated to share what I had just felt.

Anika insisted, "No, really, you have a bright glow around you."

"Then it must be more than my imagination. No sooner had I completed one round of the *Gayatri Mantra* than I felt my head light up with golden light, charging through me. Then it carried on all the way down into my spine to the tailbone and gushed into my nerve network. I felt unable to move. Cell by cell, each one came aglow with the bright light. Then, it was as though someone poured light-golden nectar into the centre of my chest. Does that sound stupid to you?" I said, not sure if Anika's scientific background had made her cynical about intuitive or mystical experiences. Yet, I was so excited about what I had just experienced.

"Wow! No, that doesn't sound stupid. That's amazing. I just felt the tickling of the cold water," Anika said.

"I feel so energised. It's as if someone's just charged me up with an enormous battery."

"That's pretty amazing. Do you think anyone can have mystical experiences, I mean without smoking or drinking the funny stuff?" Anika asked. I laughed out loud. She was from a family where academic education was above spiritual knowledge and experience of life.

We'd only just come out of the river when the priest sent a young lad to come and get us. He had a plate of Indian sweet in his hands.

"What a stunning plate of offerings," I said.

"These are for you to offer, symbolically, as *prashaad* offerings to the Goddess Ganga," the youth said as we approached the priest who was going to conduct the morning *Ganga Aarti* ceremony.

The priest said, "I have asked the cook to make these just for you to offer Ganga Ma, as it's your first *Ganga Aarti*." He smiled at us. "One of the *ashram* workers informed me last night that you were keen to join the dawn ceremony." Ah, that answered my question, without me even needing to ask it.

"How very thoughtful of you, Maharaj," I replied, moved, as we walked barefoot closer to the riverbank, each of us carrying the plate of woven banana leaf. We also carried a small, brightly coloured clay dish holding the *ghee* lamp, a set of matches, and flowers from the *ashram* garden—a handful of fragrant white night queen or *parijat* flowers, yellow marigolds or *galgota*, yellow champa and brilliant pink rhododendrons. The tiniest silver container held milk, with which we were to make only a symbolical offering into the River Ganga, so as not to add to its pollution.

Swamiji came to join us, and the ceremony started with him reciting the hymn to the River Ganges. Others seemed to know the words and so a good hour of *bhajans* began: beautiful devotional songs accompanied by the harmonium and beats of the *tabla* drums. We each were able to hold the *ghee* lamps and circulate them in front of us, making our offering of light as well as food, milk, and flowers, being careful not to let any of it actually enter into the river. The ceremony invoked an atmosphere of sacredness and peace, bringing strangers from different corners of the earth together into one common, devotional focus.

My ablutions that morning in the River Ganges had turbo-charged me, and my day at the eye camp came and went before I could say "cataracts". I felt as absorbed as a thread going through the eye of a needle, watching the one-pointed focus of the doctors. Even in these makeshift operating tents, they organised themselves impeccably and efficiently, without fuss or complaint, and got on with the business of healing the poorest of the poor. I ran from one doctor to the other, preparing and fetching patients and surgical supplies. By the second day, I had earned the trust of the doctors and I was allowed to remain with them while they operated. This meant that the patient I was looking after felt more at ease and I would hold their hand if they were particularly nervous, or I would put them at ease beforehand.

When you give yourself to others in service, I realised, you are liberated from the petty concerns of ego. Steeped in focus, you bring forth excellence in your work. Nothing else mattered, because I was one with that moment, and then the next and the next and the one after that. Being fully present, nothing else cluttered my mind. All that remained now was to learn how to create this state, again and again, without having to bathe in the icy River Ganges at sunrise, and while back in the winter fog of London.

7

Firewalk

The second evening held much promise of something exceptional happening. I loved firewalks, and could not get enough of them. They could energise me in a way nothing else could.

In overcoming the fear of walking on glowing hot embers, a person can slow down the pulsing of the heart and sharpen their focus. To walk a firebed, you have to be unquestionably present—you either steady your senses and conquer the noise of fear, or you do not walk. If you can overcome the fear, an exceptional, ecstatic experience—perhaps even an epiphany—awaits. At the very least, the stillness that comes from being present in each moment is magical—mystical even.

This firewalk was to take place on the banks of the ancient Ganges. Nothing powerful ever happened without a spark of light or fire, and I wondered what could happen when walking on a hot bed of glinting coals combined with ancient Himalayan soil along the sacred River Ganges. I couldn't begin to imagine what might happen when this came together with the powerful, healing energy that Swamiji transmitted amidst the dynamic that had formed in our group of people—those who were there to serve.

When we arrived back at the *ashram*, the firewalk experts had already done several hours of work to bring the firebed to the right temperature. The coals had been fired up much earlier, and then allowed to burn down from a raging fire to a carpet of hot, iridescent coals. They glistened ruby-red and glinted sapphire-yellow, and merged with the orange and purple dusk of the Himalayan background. The River Ganges, which ran parallel to the firebed, reflected the flickers of blue and golden tongues of flame, which mingled with red-orange sparks that danced gleefully—inviting, and anticipating, the excitement of initiations that, this new moon, were about to grace those whose time had come.

The calm and meticulous attention to detail with which the firewalk team prepared the firebed instilled confidence in me. They knew what they were doing. Rajan, Anika and I stood at the riverbank, admiring in awe the silent, dark depths that bore many a Hindu myth and ancient secrets beneath the glossy, mirrored surface of the sacred river. Others in our group had already gathered in a circle around the firebed, observing it, and confronting their own internal conversations about walking this fire.

The glimmering coals in the shadow of the sunset casted an enchanted aura and infused me with the belief that anything I wanted to do or achieve was indeed possible. It made me feel invincible.

As the sun sank into the back and beyond of the Himalayan mountain range in the distance, and robbed us of its golden luminosity, Rajan, Anika and I stepped in and joined the circle of the twenty or so people—mostly foreigners. Nervousness and introspection permeated the silence. There was a quiet connectedness and acceptance of each other as being companion souls in this rite of passage to which we each had been called. We moved to join hands with the person either side of us, declaring a silent, non-judgemental acceptance of each other in this unusual experience. The incense-scented air mingled with the fragrance of the smoke circulating from the firebed and anointed each of us with its sacred perfume.

Despite having done firewalks before, I was excited and nervous. But, going by how I had inherently reacted in similar situations, where nerves and excitement had fought each other for supremacy, I knew that I could count on myself to let excitement triumph in the eleventh hour over any anxiety. After all, I lived to better myself, to overcome my limitations, to go where I had not gone before.

This was my life, my adventure.

As the last person arrived and took his place in the circle of would-be firewalkers, the young monk who had been directing the firebed preparations joined our circle. His scrappy, bare, hairless chest was adorned solely by the Brahmin's sacred thread, which glinted in the firelight. And his light yellow cotton *dhoti* cloth, tied to his waist, draped gracefully around his spindly, lanky legs. The Brahmin monk chanted the *mantra*, *"Aum hreem namah Shivaya"*, to invoke the fierce grace of Lord Shiva, the *yogi* of *yogis*. Later, as I discovered the deeper meanings of Vedic *mantras*, I learnt that Shiva is the higher consciousness, the true and essential Self that resides in us all. Hreem, a seed sound, is a *mantra* to dispel illusion and grant liberation from the suffering that arises from the constant cycle of life and death.

As the monk chanted, he was joined one by one by the others in our group: *"Aum hreem namah Shivaya"* or "I honour the inner Self, I honour that which I am capable of becoming". The *mantra* came and wrapped itself around my tongue, gripping me in its enchanting embrace, each chant easing me into a concentration that slowly intensified into meditation with eyes wide open.

The monk in the yellow cotton wrap walked around the circle, listening to our breathing. He came up to me. While he listened to mine, he placed his hand on my belly, beckoning me to deepen my breath, to take in long, slow, full breaths and release smooth, conscious exhales. As I practiced this breathing technique, a couple of drummers with their two-headed Indian drums, the *dhol* and *mridangam*, walked around, circling behind us. The hairs on my arms rose to attention as the drums thrummed, and my heartbeat synchronised with their beat, and the steady collective chanting of *Aum hreem namah Shivaya* coursed new excitement, alertness and vitality into me.

Though on a fine knife-edge of nervous excitement, my body was steady and my mind as solid as a rock. I didn't know what lay on the other side of the walk, but I could wait no longer. It was time. It was time to 'just do it'. I was ready.

Just as I was about to let go of Anika's hand and take my place at the head of the firebed, she tugged at me. "Oh, *bap re!*" she said in my ear in Gujarati, terrified. "This looks scary, *yaar*, really scary! I don't think I can go through with this." Her Indian–English sing-song accent got stronger with her fear. I looked at her, surprised. She was visibly panicked.

"Hey, these guys are good. They'll guide you through exactly what to do when your time comes. Just breathe and chant the *mantra*. Calm your breath and let the *mantra* take you over," I replied. "Trust yourself, Anika. Listen to the instructions about what to do and what not to do, and then trust yourself and your body. It knows exactly what to do."

"I *am* trusting myself! I'm a doctor! I'll get burnt! I know I'll get burnt!" she whimpered as she tried to flash the 'I'm a doctor, trust me' card.

"Trust yourself, Anika!" I said, putting my arm around her. "This might be the reason you've really come here, to learn to trust yourself, to see that you are more powerful than you can ever imagine."

"I'm obviously not very powerful."

"Of course not," I said, before I could stop myself. "We Indian women have been punished again and again for centuries not to express anything that resembles power. I'm not talking about the aggressive, physical, macho kind of power, but the stuff that's inherent in the fabric of our real nature—that deep inner strength— that silent place that's the wellspring of authentic confidence."

Anika just looked at me like a wide-eyed rabbit under the claws of the hawk.

"Look, Anika, consider just for a moment that you have no idea who you really are."

She resisted. "But you don't know who I am. I mean, we've just known each other for a few days."

"Ah, but the more important question is, do *you* know who you are, what you're capable of, beyond what you've been made to believe?" I asked. "I may not know your habits or your personal preferences, but your inherent essential nature broadcasts itself all the time to anyone who's able to hear it. Anyone who's remotely open to perceiving beneath that 'sweetness and light' veneer of yours can see that there's a passionate, exuberant tigress just waiting to be unleashed." I said it somewhat tongue in cheek, but it was also what I saw about Anika: a huge untapped, strong inner reserve.

She had the classic demeanour of a middle class, well brought-up Indian maiden moulded by what was acceptable in our culture, conditioned into being 'a good girl'—sweet, good humoured and talkative, hard-working, intelligent and obedient—with just enough modern opinions so as to never come across as demure or dependent. She had perfected her demeanour so that there was nothing about her that would be threatening to men's egos, or women's, for that matter. Her exuberance and outward display of feminine charm or power, that would make her in any way a challenge to either gender, had been shut down over time and firmly suppressed.

"Yes, yes, you're just making this all up so you can have some company when you walk," she said dismissively, and whining in a fashion that I couldn't bear. "I know very well who I am and all that."

"Well, then, walk the fire and find out what more you're capable of," I said. "And prepare to have your mind blown open."

The Brahmin monk in a yellow *dhoti* wrap raised his hand and the drummers softened their beat so that we could hear him. "There is nothing to be afraid of. You will know when it is your turn to walk. Whenever you're ready, come to the top of this firebed and wait for the person walking to complete his or her walk. Let him come fully away from the fire. Let him dust his feet here." He indicated a spot at least seven feet away from the end of firebed.

"With one hand, swipe the sole of one foot and then the other to ensure that there are no live embers stuck to your feet." He walked back to the entrance of the firebed. "I will walk first. Remember, this is a fire*walk*, not a sprint!" He looked around at the nervous faces circling the firebed. "No running, no sprinting, no going back once you've entered the fire. No screaming, no ra-ra-ra jubilation. Keep your *drishti*, your gaze, ahead at a fixed point that's a few feet after the firebed ends. Do not look down at the firebed. Keep looking ahead," he said. "Remember, listen to your inner call. That's when you walk. Not a moment before. Let your inner call impel you to act." His English was excellent. "If you don't walk today, that's fine too. Let this be an initiation in listening, *really listening*, to what's calling forth from within."

He led us in resuming the chant, *Aum hreem namah Shivaya*. The drummers picked up their fear-busting rhythm and the monk prepared to take his first steps into the fire. Then, with a full intake of breath, he marched onto the hotbed of glassy red, orange and gold. He moved like a gazelle, and his nimble strides made him look like he was floating. It wasn't that his feet did not touch the ground, because they were firmly walking on the fire, but something in him had lifted off the earth.

Swamiji had come by earlier and invited us to collaborate and align our collective intent for successful completion of the twenty-feet-long firewalk. "Surrender yourself to healing. Allow whatever is ready for healing to float to the surface of your consciousness. Trust your inner Self," he had said, and then disappeared into the background.

This was a lesson in making a commitment, then focusing on the end goal and taking confident, brisk strides towards it, no running, no screaming, no drama—merely faith that your body knew what to do and trusting your mind to stay on course and, above all, letting go of everything else.

Five people had walked and I was itching from the start to take my turn. I couldn't wait any longer. It was my turn. This was it. Rajan's hand squeezed mine, hot and damp, but I couldn't focus on him. I had to break my hold and make my way to the head of the firebed.

As I walked to it, anticipation filled my every cell. I had no idea what the anticipation was related to, but I knew I was ready to let go—to surrender into the fire that which most suppressed me at this time. *"I let go of my heaviness. I am light, I am free, I am healthy, I am joyful."* I found myself repeating this affirmation in my mind, to my Inner Diamond, while my lips uttered, *Aum hreem namah Shivaya.*

Now that I was directly in front of the firebed, it looked terrifyingly long, much longer than the twenty feet I had been told it was. Its ferocious, shimmering redness beckoned me to step in. It was in that moment that I might have flinched and stepped back, despite my eagerness to walk, because my nerves were now as alive with anticipation as they had ever been. Without any more hesitation, I stepped onto the flaming hot carpet of coals. Its heat rose to greet and envelope me. The crunchy embers beneath my bare soles set my nervous system ablaze with deep tingling, which raced into every nook and cranny of my being, top to toe to fingertip. Red-hot electricity pulsed through every nerve and every synapse—my spine a rod of ignited brilliance. I kept striding forward. *I am light, I am free, I am healthy, I am joyful*, rang like an autonomous loop in my head. I was on fire! I felt awake, alight, ecstatic.

My walk came to an end all too quickly, with not a burn in sight, not even a singe—merely a sense of being centred, exhilarated. Every cell in my body was alive, vibrating with vitality. The massive energy that it normally took to keep myself together at all times was now otherwise channelled in this ancient medium of healing. All my defences were diminished, leaving me peacefully vulnerable. Something had been stirred deep within.

Anika was last-but-one to walk. She still shook with nervousness, but she also felt the pull to walk. She was in that classic bind between heart and mind. Her heart wanted to cause a breakthrough, but her head kept talking her out of it. Coming from a family of doctors and engineers, she had been taught to value, above all else, the workings of her mind, at the cost of the wisdom of the heart.

"You'll be so delighted when you've done this," I said, taking her hand. She steadied herself, then stepped onto the firebed. I walked alongside the fire with her, ready to join her at the other end. Anika walked as though, suddenly, she was another person—one with prowess. As she reached the end of her walk and stepped off, she trembled with shock and exhilaration.

"Did I really do that?" she asked, incredulous. "I really didn't think I could do that!" She sobbed. "Did I really do that? I never thought it was in me." This was a big accomplishment for all of us, but especially for Anika, and one that would make her proud of herself every time she thought about it.

I gave her a huge hug and asked, "What have you seen about yourself, now that you've done it?"

"You know, I felt a surge of power unleash in me as I walked on the firebed. It was right there in my belly, all along, and it just exploded, all the way into my chest and head, as if it's just been waiting to be liberated, just like you said. It's true, it's just not how I know myself to be. That's just amazing!" She sobbed and gushed with the release of potent pent-up emotions as well as inner power.

"Shall we walk one more time? This time, let's do it together." I wanted to make sure she would never doubt herself as a one-hit wonder. She looked at me, shooting me a fearful look, and curled back, as was her conditioning, when challenged to be bigger than she believed herself to be. Then she realised she had reacted this way automatically, unconsciously, and took the hand that I held out to her. Together, we walked up to the top of the firebed.

"We owe it to ourselves to do what makes us proud of ourselves, don't you think?" I giggled. "And then do them frequently." Hand in hand, we stepped into the glowing embers and walked the walk of liberating our own fire within.

In the excitement, neither of us noticed that another doctor who had come with us from Rajkot had his own misgivings about the firewalk. He was such a confident and bullish man that it never occurred to me that he might have concerns about doing the firewalk. Just as Anika and I had jointly walked to the top of the firebed, this doctor, the last one to go, was about to step forward into the fire but in the smallest split of a moment, he stepped back, turned his back to it, head hanging, and walked away limply. I went after him but he shook me off, desperate with embarrassment. I let him walk away towards the *ashram*, wanting to give him some time and space. I felt sad that we, as a group, had failed him, being consumed with ourselves.

After the firewalk, and before the *satsang* gathering of the second night, we had dinner in the *ashram* canteen, a simple mung bean and basmati rice steam-cooked *khichdi*. The rice was spiced with saffron, a pinch of turmeric, and flavoured with salt, and shallow-fried roasted cumin seeds. There was a light yellow Gujarati *kadhi*, a soup of yoghurt diluted with water, whisked until smooth. It was then boiled for at least half an hour with some gram flour to give it consistency and flavour. It had turmeric powder to give it colour and healing properties, and salt, chopped green chillies and ginger chopped into small cubes. The secret ingredient to a good Gujarati *kadhi* was always a stem or two or three of *neem* leaves, depending on the quantity. This took the dish from being a simple comfort food to being something exotic, fit for a *maharajah's* meal.

These were Gujarati staples and it made the party from Rajkot less homesick. And there was healing power in a good *khichdi* and *kadhi*, eaten with a dollop of fresh, good quality *ghee* butter. It was light, yet filling, and had a good mix of protein with carbohydrates. Its simple ingredients, when combined, had the power to heal the sick. The British of the *Raj* loved *khichdi* so much they adopted it as a part of their diet, calling it *khedgeree*.

The main *ashram* hall filled up fast while Anika, Rajan and others were having dinner, talking animatedly about the firewalk, and coming back down to earth from the exhilaration of such an unusual peak experience.

"There's even more people today in the hall than last night," Bharat, one of the volunteer doctors from the Rajkot team, said. "You guys had better hurry up and find a place to sit, otherwise you'll have to stand for the night. Oh, and Smita, the Swamiji's told me to tell you that you're not to hide in the corner this evening. You'd better find somewhere to sit towards the front." We hurried up finishing our dinner and rushed into the hall, where we found just enough space for the three of us to sit on the floor near the front.

"Swamiji's really on my case, isn't he? Have I done something wrong? Why does he want me at the front?" I asked, a little perturbed. I had already forgotten the realisation of yesterday, that this was a positive thing—an Indian courtesy.

"No, quite the opposite. He's taken you under his wing. Many people give their right arm for a *guru* of

Swami Shivananda's calibre to grace them that way."
Rajan said. "Maybe there's something about today's
discourse that's relevant to you, especially."

I felt intrigued. My default position was to react
defensively when being commanded to do something,
so I had to let it go and change the way I saw this. Rajan's
context, that the Swamiji had taken me under his wing,
was much more empowering and useful, so I accepted
it. After all, what did I have to defend anyway? Being
open to learning something new, to being guided—for
once—might prove useful.

Later, when we were on the train heading back to
Rajkot, Swamiji would explain to me that he had 'seen'
that I would be coming from London and that he would
help me. "You were already connected to me, even as
you were being born. I have been expecting you," he
said. I didn't know that Swamiji, as well as being a man
of learned knowledge, was a seer. "It is my sacred duty
to guide you and teach you whatever I can."

"The true purpose of an *ashram* is to bring seeking
souls together, like a loom that weaves many threads
into one fabric. That's why I'm very happy to answer
all the questions of each and every person, because it is
their destiny that has brought them to me."

"Nimmittamatram bhava," he said, elaborating, "I'm a mere instrument, as will you be, in due course."

Only, I was a long way from knowing in what way I might meaningfully serve others.

"In the world of 'maya' or illusion
and
'leela', the play of life,
what you see is not necessarily
the truth.

Look deeper and discern
what your mind is telling you."

8

Being Human

"The *Atma* is hidden in all and does not shine, but its subtlety is seen by people with a bright and clear intellect, says the *Kathopanishad*, 1.3.12," Swamiji recited in Sanskrit, without any book to read from and following with the English translation.

He elaborated, "Just as a diamond is buried under layers of earth that have built up over millennia, so over our lifetimes the pressures of daily life build up layer upon layer of impressions from our experiences, good and bad. These *samskaras* or psychological impressions, deeply buried memories that often inform how we behave in the present life, obscure our own radiance. These layers keep us from experiencing the radiance of the Inner Diamond. Without the light of *Brahman*, which shines through your Inner Diamond, you can't see the light for the mud. You can't see what's real and what's not. So, over time, you begin to believe that the layers of mud are what life is really about with occasional glimpses of brightness." Swamiji scanned each of our faces for clues of how we were receiving his words.

I glanced around me and the faces I saw looked blank, yet I felt hot and uncomfortable as the Swamiji's gaze came to rest on me. As he did so, it seemed to get hotter and hotter in the room, and I still radiated a glow from the firewalk. I shuffled about on my cross-legged seat, unable to remove the lock of his gaze. As Swamiji held my gaze, like a volcano about to erupt, I felt a violent surge of old emotions and familiar feelings, most of which must have been locked away in the back and beyond of my psyche and the key thrown out. What I had dealt with during my meditations in London was different to my experience now. There, I had cleared the trauma of breaking away from a thick tradition and leaving home.

Here, what I had to deal with was different. The emotions and feelings gushing to the surface were the unarticulated desolation of a child's agony and anguish that she didn't have the ability to describe. Only witness. It was the agony of seeing my poor mother forgetting who she was, of seeing her walk the streets with her hair matted. Ablaze like a black fire in the hot summer loo wind blowing through our dusty desert-like town; feeling utterly powerless to help her. The sorrow of being convinced that I was a burden on my parents; melancholy grief that my birth had something to do with my mother's illness. Did something push her over the edge when I had been born? Was her illness my fault?

Was I, somehow, bad luck? ... "She brings with her bad *karma*..." Was it true, when I was a little girl, what I had heard visiting relatives whispering among themselves? Sadness from feeling that nobody really understood my mum's condition, moreover, that no one really cared to understand it, that no one understood me, that all of this was just an inconvenience for people. Anger and disappointment that people, in general, were just self absorbed—that somehow, to different degrees, most people behaved as if the world revolved around their wants and needs, without a concern for anyone else. How could this make a fulfilling life? Sadness, anger, and fear alchemised into an outpouring of uncontrollable tears that poured involuntarily out of my eyes.

This was the suffering that the Swamiji had talked about the previous evening. He was right. I was indeed suffering, and I wondered if I was the only one in that room.

The Swamiji continued to smile at me, as he saw the tears rolling down my hot, pink cheeks; years of anguish and unbearable heartache stashed away from everyday reach, that no one had understood and that even I had been unable to make sense of.

He held me in a compassionate embrace even while being fifteen feet away. He spoke softy, "You see, our suffering comes from misunderstanding our own nature. We are not designed to suffer. We suffer because we do not understand ourselves, and therefore, others. We think we have to work towards being happy, but how can you be not happy when you are already *Sat Chit Ananda* - Pure Being, Consciousness, Bliss? When your natural state is that of an awakened, conscious, blissful being." He paused and looked around the room. "When you can embrace your fear, your pain from disappointments and heartbreak, and look calmly and steadily into the eye of the tiger, then it dissipates and, like a puff of smoke, disappears into thin air. Then, that issue will alter so much that it will not bother you again."

He got up, walked over to me, and placed his hand on my head, a calming balm on inflamed wounds. "Be blessed. Be free."

The orange-robed *guru* smiled directly at me with his bright, kind eyes. I wondered what it was about his being that had layers upon layers of old, unarticulated heaviness lift from my subconscious. I noticed that some of it made itself known in my awareness as it floated away, once and for all, from my being. Some of it merely impressed itself on me through the feelings that came and went within moments. Perhaps much of my pain and grief had come from not just what I had seen and known in my own life, but from the heavy thoughts and beliefs I had absorbed from others, from cultural conditioning. It was as if some of the pain we feel is collective and, in my becoming aware of it, I made space for it to shift for others too. Amidst all the things that we were told to believe, and that are supposed to be true and real, with all the conditioning that comes with just being born human, how could we know who we really are beneath it all?

"Being human is a privilege. It is the pinnacle of existence in a body," the old Swamiji continued, smiling as he looked at individual faces in the room. "Appreciate this as a privilege, being spirit in a human body. Use your individual God-given talents to serve others."

The kindness he transmitted through his demeanour and words made my heart spin open.

"Come from the deep inner feeling, *bhava*, of being of service and without being fixated on reward. This is perhaps the most relevant teaching in our modern age of the *Bhagavad Gita*. Know, however, that the law of *karma* is not lost on anyone. It makes rewards inevitable."

Alight with inspiration by the value that I had seen in just two days of providing 'selfless service', the conundrum had taken hold on me as to how to engage fully in the material world while remaining consciously connected to the essential Self. How I could be of service to people: integrating the seeming paradox of working without becoming fixated on selfishly motivated reward—how to work so that it becomes a source of fulfilment; taking action fearlessly as an offering to God or service to your own higher Self, or to a fellow human being. To be fully committed to the results but, at the same time, doing so not in order to get something in return, but for its own sake. This was a big ask, a big task, and though I did not yet have the answers, Swami Shivananda had facilitated an epiphany for me that would serve to change my life in the years to come.

This gem of a teaching from the ancient sages had such power over me that it triggered a whole other enquiry. How would it be to engage in a relationship or love wholeheartedly but without becoming dependent or having demanding expectations? What if you could be generous with people and let go of the notion that they had to treat you in some particular way? For example, that they had to be generous back or even just nice to you, or whatever your version of the expectation might be? What if you could conduct yourself from the context of being true to yourself, doing something or being some way because it was who you chose to be, and not being restricted by your need of how the other person should react to you?

My attention came back to the room and I heard the Swamiji say, "Being selfless, in work and relationships, demands that you take responsibility for your thoughts and actions, so that when expectation does arise, you recognise it, acknowledge its hold on you, and then let it go, restoring yourself once again to the context of selfless service, *nishkama karma*."

He looked at me once again. I was now calmer and felt cooler than perhaps ever before. "The way you hold things in your mind, how you perceive them, the frame of reference inside of which you think makes the difference between experiencing suffering or joy and happiness, this is the *ananda* part of *sat, chit, ananda*. In the world of *maya* or illusion and *leela*, the play of life, what you see is not necessarily the truth. You have to be willing to look deeper, to discern what your mind is telling you. So, be willing to take responsibility for the tricks that the mind can play to get you more fixated on the play of life and learn to navigate the mind."

"So what do I have to do to be fulfilled and at peace?" asked the angry blond American who had dialogued with Swamiji last night.

The *guru* replied, "Paul, the secret is that there is nowhere to get to. You are already there. *Sat Chit Ananda*—that is your true nature. That is *Brahman*.

Rather than engage in even more activity and have even more possessions, the key is to experience your inherent sparkle. Accept life exactly as it is and as it is not. Because, remember what the mystical psychologist Carl Jung said, what you resist persists. As you do this, you connect with stillness and peace within, and your perspective alters to make inner freedom and happiness possible." He paused as he scanned the faces of people in the room soaking in this existential wisdom. You could hear a dead fly drop.

"This inner stillness brings about a sense of dynamic peace and in that sense of peace, you can feel the magnificent presence of the sparkling Diamond that's at your core." His eyes twinkled.

Paul's face and his demeanour looked different today. It was as if his mind was melting.

"The ancient Indian seers saw at the core of the human being a brilliant, inextinguishable light, like a sparkling diamond. They called this diamond *Atman*, higher consciousness. It's also *Brahman*, *Atman* being a subset of it, if you like. *Brahman* is the macrocosm, so vast and abstract that the human mind can't relate to it. *Atman* is the higher Self and it lives within us in its essence, and that's the Diamond that I'm talking about. They saw it as the bright, supreme aspect within us that exists outside of time as we know it. It exists in the now and, therefore, the seers said that it is infinite, having no beginning and no end. Like a diamond, it lives on eternally, but as consciousness. You can imagine that there is an aspect to us that holds all the questions that we could ever ask. At the same time, it has all the answers to these questions. It also holds knowledge of every dilemma that you could face and it has an infinite repository of solutions."

Swamiji took a sharp intake of breath and closed his eyes for a moment, as if seeing something in his mind's eye.

"Close your eyes for a moment and imagine this. Imagine this Diamond exists in you. Feel it in the right side of your heart. As you see it, feel its presence, allow it to expand from a tiny little diamond into a bigger and bigger one. Let its brightness spread in you, let its brilliance cast over you, fullness, a state of being whole and complete, lacking nothing. Allow the Diamond's sparkle to touch you in those moments when you're down or low in energy. It's this Diamond that you are at one with when say, you're witnessing a picture-perfect sunset bursting with vibrant colours—orange and peach melting into pinks and purples. That moment when you first look into the eyes of your newborn baby and you are overwhelmed with a joy that is so indescribable that it alters you forever. When you're focused on doing a piece of work in which you're so absorbed that you forget the time. It felt to you like ten minutes but actually three hours have flown by. When you have woken up with an inspiring new idea or get an 'aha' moment when you're driving, you know that you have tapped into a stream of higher consciousness and engaged with it. These are moments of perfect awareness, or what the sports psychologists call 'the zone', when you are a totally at one with yourself, only the self you are one with is *Atman*, the higher Self."

Swamiji led us through this visualised meditation. I was there, with the Inner Diamond.

He continued to quote from his prolific knowledge of the ancient texts. "*Sarvam khalvidam brahma*, indeed all is *Brahman*', says *Chandogyopanishad*, III, 1.4.1. The Inner Diamond or higher Self is part of the pure consciousness from which all of life springs, the higher intelligence, and the field that gives birth to all of what is possible. In the West, you talk of the Divine. The ancient sages called it *Brahman*."

He looked around the room at people still deep in meditation, enticed by the beauty of the Inner Diamond, not wanting to open their eyes to the world outside. The concepts he taught were complex. How did they relate to us as human beings? What was the link between the ego, the higher Self, and *Brahman*—the cosmic field of consciousness? I wanted to make sure that I didn't misunderstand them, so I raised my hand to seek clarification.

I asked, "Can you please tell me if I'm understanding this correctly? Would it be fair to say that *Atman*, the higher Self, is the individual spark of *Brahman* and like the bridge of higher consciousness that connects to human beings? Say, a bit like how a mother connects to her unborn baby through an umbilical cord, granting it life? Does the higher Self, *Atman*, connect to the human body and its ego by sending down a spark of itself in the human body?"

The Swamiji confirmed, "That's a good way of putting it."

"And the soul, is that the spark of the higher Self? Is that what the ancient seers called the *jiva-atman*? Would that be the spark that breathes life and divinity into our humanity?"

"'*Anor aniyan mahato mahiyam, Atmasya jantor nihito guhayam*; smaller than the teeniest particle, larger than the infinite expanse, the soul lives hidden in the human heart'. So it says in *Kathopanishad 1.2.20*. 'The

Atma is hidden in each of us and isn't visible. Subtle though it is, it is seen through the bright intellect,' says *Kathopanishad, 1.3.12*. The soul, *jiva-atman*, is indeed the link that connects the human being to his higher Self." He nodded, pleased that someone was getting it.

Then, summarising, he quoted *Mundaka Upanishad, 3.1.7*, "That (*Brahman*) is brilliant, immense, inconceivable, subtler than the subtle. It's far beyond what is far and yet near and found in the cave of the human heart."

"All these things sound like really complex concepts. If I don't understand them, does it mean that I won't be able to have inner freedom or peace?" the Dutchman from last night's gathering asked.

"That's a very good question!" Swamiji replied. "The answer is, no, you don't have to understand them. You just have to know that you are a part of the mighty consciousness and that its nature is joy and bliss— *ananda*. If you can accept that, then it will begin to make itself known to you in a way that makes sense to you. See, it's like this, you don't have to speak Japanese if you want to go for a year of travel in Japan. You could go anyway and you'll have a good time. Just because you don't speak Japanese doesn't mean you can't go to Japan. You can go anyway. But if you learned to speak a bit of

Japanese, about the people there, about their traditions, and so on, would it help to enrich your experience of Japan?"

"Possibly," Bart, the Dutchman, said. "But it sounds too much like hard work!" People laughed.

Swamiji joked. "Yes, enlightenment shouldn't be hard work, should it." He became serious again and continued, "Look, the Gita is very clear about this. You can become enlightened through devotion or *bhakti*. You can undertake *nishkama karma* or selfless service and that too will liberate you. You might take on both ways at the same time and also learn through knowledge. Something has brought you here this evening and I'm sharing with you the paths that I have chosen to for myself."

Bart nodded and carried on listening.

"In order to understand how, as a human being, you can have freedom from suffering and be powerful in life, it is important to understand, or least know, that there are the seen and unseen layers of our consciousness. The *Bhagvad Gita*, one of ancient India's spiritual treasures, explains that there are three main layers of our consciousness. It gives us excellent insights into the workings of the ego, the lowest layer that is our personality or identity and what we call 'human'. It explains the nature of our higher Self, *Atman*, or the Diamond, as being a fragment of the highest layer, as being pure consciousness, *Brahman*. 'He (*Brahman*) is incandescent and transparent; he exists both without and within; unborn, without *prana*, without mind, pure and grander than the grandest, he is indestructible.' So says the *Mundaka Upanishad, 2.1.2.*" Swamiji placed his hands together and brought the talk to a close.

9

Mining the Diamond

On the third evening, Paul—the American—asked Swamiji, "You said that there is a diamond within us or that we are diamonds. But why don't we see it or feel it, then?"

Swamiji smiled. "It's a very good question. Just as a diamond is buried under layers of earth that has built up over millennia, so over our lifetimes the pressures of daily life build up layer upon layer that obscure our own radiance. These layers keep us from experiencing the radiance of the Inner Diamond."

"But aren't diamonds created under extreme pressure and can take millions of years to form and come to the surface? I mean, without the pressure of the earth and the right temperature conditions, the carbon atoms would not become a diamond."

"Exactly," Swamiji picked up. "A newly extracted diamond, when it has just been mined, is covered in layers and layers of old, compacted rock-like mud. It does not look like a diamond at all. It does not shine or sparkle. It has to be cleaned and polished for the lustre of the diamond to emerge. Every diamond takes millions of years to form and become the jewel that will eventually adorn a delighted woman's new wedding ring or be installed at the cutting edge of a drill."

I was still gobsmacked that Swamiji was talking about the diamond, *my Inner Diamond!* How could I have known about its existence—even seeing and experiencing it as a seven-year-old in front of Grandma Motima's home shrine? Where did I know it from? How come I even called it the Inner Diamond?

"So, are you saying that just as a diamond forms over millions of years of pressure, we too need a certain amount of tension, pressure, and stress, perhaps in the guise of setback, dissatisfaction, disappointment, unhappiness, sadness, and disillusionment, before we will look within ourselves to find our Inner Diamond? Is that what you're saying?" Paul asked, deep in enquiry.

"Something like that. We don't need that sort of psychological pressure, but you might be more inclined to go soul searching when something in your life triggered you to do so. I mean, when life's giving you everything you want, do you care about God or looking for fulfilment?"

"Hell, no! I'd be too busy enjoying myself in some bar in Venice, California!"

"Here's the distinction," Swamiji explained, leaning in Paul's direction. "The difference between earthly diamonds and the Diamond within is that the *Atman* at the core of each of us is already fully formed, in full sparkle and radiance. It is waiting, patiently, for your awareness to locate its presence and claim it your prize. All it takes is clearing away the debris within the mind that obscures its existence."

He looked at Paul and nodded his head, Indian-style, bobbing it on his neck side to side as if the neck were a spring.

"So that's why it helps to understand your own nature?" Paul asked.

"Precisely." The *guru* was in his element. "The nature of the Inner Diamond is radiance and brilliance. It's your inherent power and knowledge. It is your joy and bliss."

As Swamiji explained the nature of the Inner Diamond, I felt validated and gratified, because my experience of it was just as he was describing it.

"That's the place of genius too," he continued. "When things are going well in life, when life is flowing with ease (even though it might take focus and hard work), you are in alignment with your Inner Diamond. You are in the flow of what is inherently appropriate to your natural design. You are being 'true to yourself'. Only, the self that you are being true to is your higher Self. And yet, when you are winning and things are going your way in life, there is little reason to look inside yourself for it. And the ego, your me-me-me, is happy to take the credit for the success. Yet the Inner Diamond is powering you at all times. It, unlike the ego, does not need to take or be given credit. It just is." Though he was looking at Paul, Swamiji was addressing and blowing open the mind of every person in the room.

"If the Inner Diamond is so central and powerful, I mean ... what you're saying is that this Diamond's what gives life lustre ... then why then do we wait for setbacks, disappointments, and disillusionment before we turn within ourselves for solutions?" Paul asked.

"That's a very intelligent question," Swamiji bounced back. "Why indeed? Would it not be more intelligent to locate the source of our power when the going's good so that we can avoid unnecessary setbacks, disappointments, and disillusion? It would seem obvious that prevention is better than the cure, wouldn't you agree?" Swamiji raised his hand and turned his palm toward himself, as if he was twisting in a light bulb, a classic Indian body language when asking a question.

Again, he looked around the room, pausing to let this thought sink in before resuming his commentary. "While the diamond needs to be mined from the many layers of earth, we need to cut through the layers of our own mind that keep us shielded from the perfectly formed Diamond that is already at our core. The ancient Indian seers said that we are the spark of *Brahman*, the super consciousness that is the source of creation of the universe and that is infused in absolutely everything around us, including you, Paul. The Diamond in you has been shaped by pure consciousness."

Paul spoke up again while the *guru* paused for a sip of water. "There is a theory that not all diamonds are shaped by compression of the earth, but that some have been shaped inside the core of ancient stars. It's a fact that gold, iron, oxygen, and carbon too, have been formed by ancient stars long gone and that they have reassembled in the fabric of our planet. These long-gone stars, that were the first and second generation of stars in our universe, gave us the building blocks of life as we know it."

Swamiji responded, enthused, "And we are made of these same elements, and we see the evidence all around us that we are made of ancient stardust. Current scientific thinking is that our sun is a third-generation star. This means that two generations of stars have had to explode to form our solar system. It would therefore be fair to say that we are, literally, sentient stardust and you are truly a diamond!"

Paul was now getting the conversation. He encapsulated it by saying, "Just as the baby floats inside its mother's womb, so the *Atman* floats in the pure consciousness of *Brahman*. Just as the baby is a spark of its mother, so the Inner Diamond is the spark of pure consciousness. You, the person with your name, your body, your life, are a material manifestation of this consciousness. You are therefore not just your body and the identity that you know yourself to be. You are indeed much, much, much more besides. Is that it?"

"Very fairly put." Swamiji summed it up, "The field of all creative potential holds silent seeds of what is possible to bring into material reality. The ancient seers of India said that all questions, all answers, all problems, all solutions, all past, and all futures are held in *Brahman*, this space of nothingness that can give birth to absolutely anything. And yet, though it can hold all of these, it exists purely in the light of the now moment.

Your Inner Diamond is connected to this field of pure potentiality. That's where you go to find the answers to your dilemmas."

Paul shared his insight, jokingly, "To rediscover the power of your Inner Diamond, you do not need the heavy machinery that diamond miners use to drill into the layers of earth, but the laser beam of your own awareness to clear away the layers of the erroneous beliefs and unhelpful conditioning that are keeping to from your view."

There was a chuckle in the room as people visualised Paul's imagery. Anika gave me a cheeky nod in approval. I think she was warming to Paul.

Bart, the Dutchman, was again restless. He shouted out his question without being invited by Swamiji, "But to achieve what you're talking about, your mind would have to be as still and silent as Lake Lucerne on a quiet day. That's never going to happen, because it's virtually impossible."

"Well, that's a very valid remark and in chapter two of the *Bhagavad Gita*, Arjun, the brave warrior, asked Lord Krishna a very similar question," Swamiji replied.

"Really? Wow. And what did Krishna say?" the Dutch fellow asked.

"He replied that self control is the key, that without it you cannot have a steady mind, and steady mind gives rise to intelligence. With a mind that is turbulent like a sea in a storm, how can it be possible to find peace?" Swamiji smiled knowingly at the Dutchman. "Have you ever been happy when your mind is at unrest?"

"Of course not. I see what you mean," Bart replied, a little more quietly now.

"So, Lord Krishna's point was that a calm, peaceful mind gives rise to the intelligence that lies within, you see." Swamiji bobbed his head again in delight.

10

Mind Monkeys

"**B**eware and be aware of the fluctuations of the negative mind," the Swamiji continued the next day.

"You will have heard the saying, 'It's all in the mind'? There is a Sanskrit teaching, *Yad Bhavam Tat Bhavati*—you become what you think. In the Yoga tradition, the mind is said to exist in two states, the gross and the subtle. It's the chattering mind, the negative mind, or the mind that makes you feel unhappy. I will also refer to the gross mind as the chattering mind."

He looked at a woman sitting in the back row then carried on, as if talking to her. "Let's call these emotions, feelings and thoughts, 'mind monkeys'. They live in the dense forest of the gross mind and ceaselessly jump from branch to branch, or thought to thought, playing havoc inside your head. *Yogis* call this activity the 'fluctuations of the gross mind', while psychologists call it 'interior dialogue' or 'internal conversation'. Let's just call it 'mind monkey chatter', because doing so immediately reminds you that these thoughts are trivial and, more often than not, unreliable. More importantly, it reminds you that acting on the basis of such internal conversation is usually unwise and counter productive."

The woman he'd addressed asked in a soft voice, "Swamiji, may I ask a question?" Swamiji smiled and bobbed his head side to side in approval.

"Mind monkeys, are they a part of our ego?" she asked. Her manner was confidant yet respectful, and distinct from that of the Westerners who had earlier asked questions of the Swamiji. She showed deference and it did not detract from her sense of self.

"Yes, indeed. They are a product of the ego mind. The monkeys create havoc and constant chatter in the mind. What is your name, young lady?" Swamiji asked.

"Roshni, Swamiji," she replied, granting him esteem. It would have been considered rude to address such a senior man, let alone a monk of a high order without adding the *'ji'* at the end of Swami. Suffixing *'ji'* at the end of a person's title or name was a mark of respect, much like in French, where you would address a parent or elder or someone you were less familiar as *'vous'* and not *'tu'*.

"Roshni, the bright light, a beautiful name," he said warmly. "It's heartening to see so many young faces in the room tonight."

"Thank you, Swamiji. Where does the monkey mind conversation come from? What does it sound like? How can you recognise it?" Roshni asked from the back of the room.

"Parts of it filter up from what's lying in your subconscious mind, and most of it from your conscious mind. Mind monkey chatter comes from fear, and distracts and disturbs you, pulling you out of being present in the moment and into things that are to do with the past or even the future." He paused to let his words register, then continued:

"It's something that happens automatically. That is, the thoughts that arise spontaneously from this chattering are not something you consciously choose to think—they come up all by themselves, as if on autopilot. This is why it seems like you are at the mercy of these thoughts, helpless, and that you have no control over them and even act according to their promptings." He looked around the room.

Roshni delved further. "So, if it's on autopilot, does that mean you don't have any control over it, Swamiji?"

"Actually, you can, but that requires some work. However, remember, an unruly mind is not fertile ground for happiness. You can learn how to control the mind and, if you practice restraining the monkey mind long enough, you will be able to master how you interact with such thoughts and limit their destructive impact on your mood, actions, and on the choices that you make," the Swami said.

I caught his emphasis that this was a conscious choice and that it takes some effort and work.

"Your mind can be your worst enemy or it can be your friend, so it says in the *Bhagavad Gita*, chapter one. Use your mind to lift you higher, not to drag you down."

He signalled that the talk was finished and moved us into the chanting of some beautiful old *mantras*, bringing this *satsang* or gathering to a close.

11

Symbols

A month after coming back from India, while driving home after work, I hit a traffic jam. Déjà vu, from a dream the night before, hit me as my eye caught the sign of a shop selling art supplies. In the dream, I saw myself painting, and I felt an inexplicable urge to go and buy painting materials.

I had never considered myself as having any artistic talent. I could barely draw matchstick figures, let alone paint, yet here I found myself with an urgent compulsion to buy brushes, paints and paper, and begin to paint. I stopped at a nearby art store, explained what I needed, and found myself returning home with art supplies galore, aquiver with excitement, anticipation and apprehension.

I had no idea what I might want to paint, because even if I knew what to paint, I wouldn't be able to—no talent, see. I began, hesitant, by just using a brush to put some splashes of colour to paper, and my suspicions were instantly and horribly confirmed, for what came out was something that even a five-year-old would be ashamed of.

It was official. I really couldn't paint. I not only realised with frustration my deep lack of talent for freehand painting, but had to endure the taunting voice of my inner critic as it mocked my pretensions.

"Stupid girl! How ridiculous are you, thinking you can paint?"

Yet despite the obvious lack of world-class talent, and the inner taunts, the yearning to use and experience colour still ran strong through me. Something within me craved expression through watercolours.

That night, in my sleep, I felt restless. Whilst I slept, my dreams revealed some of the deeper processes of my mind: I saw vivid, three-dimensional geometric forms spinning, floating around me, moving through me, or me jumping directly into them as though they were gates to some other dimension.

When I woke up the next morning, I had an 'aha' moment as I realised that what I needed to paint was not a freehand, conventional sort of painting, but something that needed to be done with geometric instruments. Though I could not yet see the image in my mind, I could almost feel it buzzing in my hand, waiting to pour out. After breakfast, I drove back to the art supplies store and bought rulers of different lengths, a compass, a set square and a protractor, a pencil and an eraser.

The first thing I did, once home again, was draw a four to five inch circle in the very centre of the A3 paper, using the compass. Then after that, something within me told me that I just had to let my hand do the work, not my conscious mind.

Let my hand do the work? Not control the process? I felt puzzled and horrified at the prospect of letting go of control.

I loved being in control of all my actions, knowing what I was doing, and why I was doing it. The prospect of freestyling with no plan, no goal, filled me with deep unease. Still, whatever was beckoning me from within didn't feel threatening, and I decided to give it a shot, if only out of curiosity.

With no preconception of what was to come next, I noticed that my mind, enslaved to this over-developed habit, was hard at work trying to figure out what to do, unwilling to let go. Once again, I decided to bite the bullet, stop trying so hard, and let my hand move to where it wanted to take me: let whatever was waiting within flow forth. It took me a while, but once I was able to let go and trust the process, I began to feel every next line and curve of the drawing emerging naturally. My mind aligned with my hand, which moved around the page fluidly. I made six semi-circles to frame the outside of the initial circle, and then some quarter circles, twelve undulating sunray-like flames, some lotus-like petals to crown the image, and then some triangles within the centre to complete the design.

My mind may have had no conscious idea of what was going on, but my hand glided around intelligently to where it wanted to go on the piece of paper. Whatever was 'asking' to be on this paper, had already been 'downloaded' into my subconscious mind, and sat there in perfect clarity, waiting for my hand to give it form and structure and make itself visible. I could not actually see the design in my mind's eye, but my hand knew exactly where it had to go.

Triangles, circles and curves had arranged themselves in perfect harmony, and formed some kind of design, which revealed itself moment by moment. I had no clue of its purpose or meaning, but just drawing it had already given me a sense of liberation.

I wasn't just drawing; I was flowing in a trance, at one with this design and whatever was guiding me. My mind and ego had stepped out of the way of this process, and given way to a deeper knowing. What I was experiencing was extraordinary, and oddly—even though my ego and my controlling, analytical mind were not in charge—I felt completely at ease, directed and centred, buzzing with clarity and energy, and free of self-judgement and internal commentary that were otherwise my constant companions.

Now that the design was visibly there on paper, I realised that the paints I had bought the night before were for putting colour to this design. Having created something so coherent, tangible and harmonious and with such ease and play, I trusted this process a little more. Once again, rather than think about what colours to apply and analyse the potential result, I just let my hand do the choosing. My eyes fell first on the ultramarine blue paint, and I used it to bring the semicircles to life. Then the cobalt blue jumped into my focus, as if saying, "Me, me, me!"

A blue-based marine was begging to join the symphony, so I splashed that into the sunray-like waves. Various aspects of my drawing blossomed with colour, which blended perfectly with each other and aroused a calm and quiet flow of delight. The simple geometry, which my mind might have earlier dismissed as simple and childlike, had turned out to be a beautiful, sophisticated design that resembled a symbol of some sort. The symbol felt strangely familiar within me, as if

I had some faint, ancient memory of it floating around in a vast ocean of consciousness, and yet I couldn't remember having seen anything quite the same as this.

I still had no idea what this symbol was or what it was for, but in allowing it to flow from me, I now knew what pure inspiration felt like. Something within me that was previously blocked had—with each stroke of the pencil and lick of colour—simply dissolved. It was as though spirit spoke directly to, and through, me in a multidimensional language I had yet to learn. This one symbol had opened up something quite profound in me. A pathway had been locked for the longest time, and the symbol I had been led to draw and paint was the magic key to unlocking it.

The first symbol was a relatively simple one and I made it within the same day. The following day, a Sunday, I couldn't wait to make another one. This process was as engaging as it was intriguing. I loved being in this trance-like state; it was absorbing, seductive, exhilarating, and I wanted to experience more of it. As I worked on one symbol, I could feel the second already lining up to broadcast itself to me as soon as I was ready for it, then the third, then the fourth and so on. Within a space of twelve months, I made more than twenty or so, each with their own unique geometry and colour combinations.

Every symbol had its own internal landscape, tapping open different dimensions of emotions and feelings, some of which felt alien to me. Some I made were truly pleasurable to make—one had me weeping with sadness for no reason at all. With another, I was a cheeky child at play, as if I was doing something that I was not supposed to. In fact, all of the symbols had an innocence about them, expressed through their open vibrant colours that implied a quiet inner joy for life. It seemed as if each symbol expressed a completely different person, or perhaps a different aspect of the same person, each having its own personality. Each symbol I painted seemed to open me up little by little. At first, its effects were unnoticeable, but after a while I became aware that every symbol I painted was like a therapy. It felt almost addictive, because making these symbols took me into a state of trance, or what the Americans call 'being in the zone', distinct from how I felt normally. I felt lighter with each symbol. The intensity that had, for years, gripped my heart centre started to loosen its hold on me. With this, there was a release of energy, a sort of inner power that emerged gradually, the likes of which I had not been aware of within myself before.

Could this be the 'treasure' that I felt buried and trapped in me? The symbols seemed to be activating aspects within me that I didn't yet know.

I laid these images on the floor of my sitting room, on the coffee table, and some were stuck on the walls with Blu Tack. I arranged them and rearranged them, this way and that, in the hope that some pattern might emerge or something about them might become apparent to me and solve the puzzle of why they were pouring through my hands. Every now and then, while drinking a cup of tea, after coming home from work or back from grocery shopping, I would reorder them, moving them from the coffee table to the wall, to see if some of them looked like they belonged next to one another, while those with a different quality about them went either above or below the central ones. I tried to see if they made more sense combined than individually, but several symbols and litres of paint later, I was just as clueless as when I had started.

Where on earth had this yearning to make these symbols sprung from? How did I know to make them? Where had I learnt about its geometry? Where had I learnt about combining colours and their effects? Why did they have such an effect on me? How could just a few lines and curves, ordered and painted in a certain combinations, make me feel so altered inside? What were these symbols? Did they mean anything? Had they a recognised place in history or did they stand alone? Or did they have relevance only for me at this time in my life? Where was I drawing them forth from? Was there a special dimension within consciousness in which such symbols held some meaning?

In surrendering to their creation, I became more still in my meditations. I had been meditating for several years but, now, I began to hear a deeper silence—a silence infused with peace. The restless jabbering of my mind monkeys quietened little by little, so that I could doubt less and trust myself more. I had no idea if what was pouring through me was a part of my own mind, or of a consciousness greater than me, that I somehow had gained access to. Whatever it was, I was as much in the dark about them, many symbols later, as I was when I made the first.

For my sixteenth symbol, I started working on one that was very different to the others. It wasn't so much the way it looked, but how it made me feel.

From the moment I drew my first stroke on this particular symbol, fear and terror of a kind that I had not experienced in my life so far, crept up within me— intense. On the two evenings I spent drawing the symbol, I had dark, disturbing dreams throughout those nights. Not usually given to remembering my dreams, I dreamt vividly on both occasions, overwhelmed with panic, and struggling, as though I was bundled up in darkness.

On waking from these dreams, I was left with a profound sense of powerlessness. On the third night, having drawn the symbol, I painted it, filling it with colour. With every few strokes of the brush, I saw flashes of blackness, pure blackness, and yet I was using a bright, prime orange with which to colour. I had to put the brush down and stop, because I couldn't bear the sense of blackness that overwhelmed me. I felt as if I was caught up in something, something big, something horrible, but nothing that I could remember.

I came to think of this painting as the Symbol of Terror.

Over the next six months, every so often I went back to see if I could do some more work on it without being overwhelmed by the feelings of panic, powerlessness and sheer darkness. I found I could only work on it for five, maybe fifteen minutes, before I felt enveloped by those eerie feelings again. I put it somewhere I couldn't see or feel it, and decided to carry on with making other symbols. For now, I had to leave the Symbol of Terror well alone, shut away in my spare room, incomplete.

Even though it was out of sight, I did not succeed in getting it out of my mind. The Symbol of Terror had a life of its own. The more I could not complete it, the more it nagged me, and filled me with inexplicable fear.

The more it troubled me, the more intrigued I became with it, gripped by the power it had over me.

It was an enigma, a mystery, that I had to find a way of solving.

"Inner stillness brings about
a sense of dynamic peace
in which you can feel
the magnificent presence
of the sparkling Diamond
that's at your core."

12

Mandalas

One cold and damp Friday evening in November, a short while after I had come home from work, a knock came at my front door. I wasn't expecting anyone, so I thought it might be my neighbour who sometimes popped in.

"Hi! What a lovely surprise. Come in." It was my friend Robert, grinning from ear to ear. He had someone with him.

"Hello! I hope you don't mind my dropping by without notice. Harish and I were passing by and I really wanted you two to meet before he flies out to the States tomorrow," Robert said.

"Of course." I invited them in. "Guests are gods," which I had heard Grandma Motima say a thousand times.

Robert and I had been friends for many years and shared in common our passion for delving into metaphysics and the mystery of being human.

"This is Harish." Robert turned to the tall, lean man with pleasant North Indian features. I wasn't expecting to see Robert, much less the man with him, and felt a little embarrassed as my apartment was strewn with all of my painted symbols, some on the floor, others blu tacked to the wall.

I was embarrassed and uncomfortable for another reason too. These paintings seemed childlike, hardly the creation of a master. Nevertheless, imperfect as they were, they had become precious to me, as if they were my babies. Not ready to subject them to opinions and criticism, I had not yet shown them to a single soul.

I beckoned Robert and Harish to go up the stairs to my first-floor apartment.

Robert said, "Harish is a scholar and a painter. He's spent a great deal of time studying the *Shastras* (ancient Indian texts) with some of India's holy men. I met him some years ago, in Thailand, of all places, while I was doing research for my PhD. I was telling him about your recent travels and experiences in India. I thought you two should meet."

On seeing my symbols, Robert, who often surprised me with his diverse knowledge, said, "Oh, wow. These are amazing. I didn't know you painted *mandalas*, Smita."

"*Mandalas*? What are they?" I asked, puzzled.

"Don't you know what *mandalas* are? Haven't you come across them while you were in India? I thought you would know them from the iconography of the Vedics. They're similar to the geometric representations of the various deities in the Indian spiritual philosophies," he said.

"Ah, yes, I've seen those, but aren't they called *yantras*? They tend to have a special square containing intricate geometric patterns, lotus petals, and so on. Aren't they more formal than my splattering of colour?" I chuckled.

Robert turned to his friend. "What do you think?" He then looked at me. "Harish has painted some stunning sacred art."

"Really? How amazing," I said, delighted at the unexpected coincidence of having someone show up in my home that might be able to shed some light on all these patterns and symbols that had been pouring out of me in the last months. "What an incredible coincidence."

As Harish and Robert were sipping the fresh spiced chai tea I had just made, Harish said, "*Yantras* are more commonly seen in Indian temples as abstract representations of certain deities. *Mandalas* are much more esoteric in that their relevance is not commonly known to everyone. In ancient times, because of their potent power, they were taught only to carefully selected pupils."

"You're right. I've heard of *yantras*, but haven't come across *mandalas*," I said. "I thought I was possessed or going mad! Never painted a thing in my life and, out of the blue, these things have started to emerge. From where or how I know to make them, I have absolutely no clue. It's as if I'm spellbound or entranced when I'm making them. It's driving me wild with curiosity as to what they are and why I'm making them ... So, what I've been painting are *mandalas*, then?"

"They certainly are. *Mandalas* can be very varied in their appearance," Harish said. "The special square you mentioned earlier that is in *yantras* is based on ancient Indian mathematics. They're vibrationally aligned to what's called the Vedic Square and created using a sacred number grid. *Mandals* are ..."

"*Mandal*—that's a circle isn't it, in Sanskrit?" I asked.

"Exactly. All *mandalas* are circular, much like your ones, and they are often sealed off by a square, or there are squares and triangles or other geometric shapes captured within a large circle, depending on what the *mandala* is representing."

Robert, alive with interest, said, "There is a line of thought that in order to bring something into manifestation from its formless essence—I mean, to give it material form—you have to square it off, otherwise it remains in its essential state, which is depicted by a circle."

"Goodness! And I thought I was just playing with shapes and colours. I am intrigued as to where I know any of this from. What more do you know about *mandalas*?"

"They've been used in various traditions—Indian and, later, Buddhist and Tibetan—as a means to focus the mind and enter into a deeper state of meditation," Harish said. "They were used to tap into dimensions of inner consciousness that lie beyond words. The ancient sage *rishis* said that there were two types of meditation or *dhyana*: *saguna* and *nirguna*. Focusing on an image, such as a *mandala*, is called *saguna*—*sa* meaning 'with' and *guna* meaning 'form'. This is because you're focusing on a form in your meditation in order to acquire the qualities and attributes imparted by that form, such as that of a deity. Whereas in *nirguna* meditation, *nir* means 'without' and *guna* means 'form'. Here you're concentrating on the formless consciousness." Harish stopped to sip some more spiced chai tea.

"That's what it's called. Swami Shivananda, in Rishikesh, mentioned something about these different approaches to meditation, but most of what he said went right over my head," I said.

"Often, being in the presence of an enlightened *guru* is less about what you learn from what is said and more about the transmission of energy that you receive through him," Harish said.

"Is one method better than the other?" Robert asked.

"Well, the formless is vast and infinite and very difficult for a meditator to grasp until his third eye is opened through various practices and regular meditation. So, then, since you have to be an advanced meditator to be able to grasp the vastness of the field of consciousness, it's much easier to meditate on some sort of form, such as an image or *mandala*, or the *guru's* voice guiding you into the inner realms," Harish said.

"That's fascinating. Are my *mandalas* ones that someone could use to meditate on?" I asked, intrigued.

"When I'm making them, I go through all different emotions, sometimes they make me feel happy and joyful, and terribly sad at other times. There's even one that's thoroughly terrorising me. Whatever the emotion, when I've completed one, I can feel that something has shifted within me, something that I didn't even know was there or needed shifting." I pondered aloud, hoping to get a little closer to solving the mystery of my *mandalas*.

"Well, *mandalas* are essentially energy patterns that put us in touch with our inner nature. They get to the parts of your inner workings that lie beyond words. They were often painted to release trapped or blocked emotional energy. Perhaps what you've been experiencing is something of a release," Harish said.

"That would so make sense. These symbols seem to be expressing something intrinsic within me. It's as if what I call the Inner Diamond is showing a part of itself to me through these vibrant, dynamic symbols that look like they might just burst off the page, come alive, and start dancing on the table!" I said, amused by the possibility.

In this unexpected conversation, I now knew that my splattering of colour had a name—they were *mandalas* and they even had a place in ancient iconography. Their mystery should have lessened by now, but for me, it only added to their enigma. Why was I, an ordinary person steeped in the business world, making them?

"I'm sure it will all become clear to you in time," Harish assured me. "Your experiences in India have perforated your awareness so that your Inner Diamond can make its presence known to you and start communicating with you more directly, more often, rather than just inklings and dreams. Think of these *mandalas* as your Inner Diamond shining its brilliance and grabbing your attention."

Little did Harish know that he was closer to the truth than any of us could have known.

Through Harish showing up at my house, I now knew that I was painting *mandalas*, that these symbols were considered sacred art, and that they were used for meditation and freeing up emotional blocks. However, there were still significant pieces of my *mandala* puzzle missing.

13

Quest

After the Christmas holidays, I settled back into my work but, since meeting with Robert and Harish, I had no further insights or realisations that satisfied my questions. They were niggling me now more than ever. Nor could I complete, or go near, the Symbol of Terror. Not being able to complete this black and orange symbol had left me dangling in an exceptionally eerie space. I felt as though I was in grave danger—in the constant grip of fear and dread of some powerful, perilous force that felt strangely familiar. And yet, this internal landscape simply did not correlate to how I knew myself to be, or of what was going on in my life.

I sensed that I needed to know why the Symbol of Terror had such power over me.

One dark, wintry January evening after work, I sat down for my daily meditation but, today, I sat with a notebook and pen, and with a specific purpose in mind. I needed to have answers, and now. I had never done a meditation quite so specific before. I intended to ask my Inner Diamond direct questions and hoped to be able to hear clear answers.

For about twenty minutes, I quietened my mind using my regular method, just observing my thoughts rising and floating away effortlessly. Only the presence of a secret *mantra* pierced my reverie. I had been initiated into it by one of the *gurus* I had met during my recent travels in India. My reward in this meditation was absorbing the delicious, blissful silence of the subtle gaps between the rising and dying away of thoughts. Then, at the end of those twenty minutes, I poured out the questions that had been bothering me for months. I asked them mentally, emphatically, but waited, still in deep trance-like meditation, with my pen poised to my notebook for the answers.

With no artistic talent or training, why was I making *mandalas* so prolifically? Why did I find them so totally riveting and absorbing? Why did the colours of these *mandalas* feel so palpable? Why did they evoke such strong emotions in me? Why did geometry feel so familiar to me, and where was this memory from? Why couldn't I complete the Symbol of Terror? Why was I so afraid with this one symbol?

Though my intent was strong, I had no guarantee that any answers would come.

What happened next was beyond even my wildest imagination. With alarming speed and clarity, my Inner

Diamond responded, *"Go to the library in Holborn in central London. Ask to see information about an admiral in the French Navy who lived in the 1800s. You will find information about him in the mathematics section, under the' J' classification."*

Goodness! I nearly levitated! That was specific. I couldn't remember ever having been given an answer so crystal clear by my Inner Diamond, so I was finding it hard to digest this one and yet, try as I might, I could certainly not have come up with this for myself. For one thing, I had never heard of a library in Holborn and thought it was probably one of the small local ones, if there was one there at all.

"But what has a navy admiral got to do with mathematics?" I asked, flabbergasted yet cynical.

"Go and see," was all the answer I got.

"What about the Symbol of Terror? Why can I not go near it anymore to finish it? Why does it fill me with such fear? Why do I feel like something terrible is about to happen?"

The questions flooded out of me, frantic for some clue to put me out of my misery.

"Go to see Chris Griscom on the 1st of April. Go and do what she is doing at that time," my Inner Diamond answered.

Once again, I was utterly astounded by this startlingly emphatic response. Who would have thought that it was possible to tap into this aspect of the self and receive such practical counsel?

"Chris Griscom? How will I get hold of her? I don't know where she will be then," I replied, flustered.

In the days well before the Internet and Google, people did not yet have their own websites to let the world know of their existence and whereabouts, so finding them could in itself be a mission.

Although Robert had lent me one of Chris Griscom's books, I had hardly read it and, during Chris's talk in London, I had barely understood what she was talking about.

"Look on the back of her book," my Inner Diamond said.

"Authors don't normally write their addresses and phone numbers on the back of books. Precisely for the very reason that they don't want strangers showing up on their doorsteps." How cantankerous was I?!? I was arguing with the wise Diamond!?!

"Look on the back of the book, call her, and go and do what she is doing on the 1st of April." The Diamond's words came with warmth and calm clarity.

Chris was based somewhere in America, but that's all the information I had. "How much will all this cost, and where will I get the money from that quickly? I've spent most of my money travelling around India for six months, and then moving into this new place." My demands sounded petulant even to me.

"The money will be there. You will have more than enough."

Then it was gone. I lost my connection and couldn't arouse any more responses.

I went to bed exhilarated and baffled, all at once. This was *not* what I'd had in mind when I had so boldly sat down with my notepad and pen. I'd had something simpler in mind—something that would bring me straightforward answers. Though for sure, I had received some answers, specific and clear as they were, they raised more questions than they answered.

Not only that, but they were a huge ask on my faith and trust, not to mention my bank account.

And yet, this interaction, this connection, was special—more than an exchange of mere words. Connecting with my Inner Diamond in this way had filled me with an unusual vitality and energy. A light and immense energy.

The next morning, my cynical mind monkeys jumped around in my head with riotous ridicule. Was I being led like a lamb to cloud cuckoo land? Was I completely losing it?

Or did I really have something remarkable and divine unfolding in my life?

I had to choose: trust or cynicism. Trust in my Inner Diamond or the cynicism of the egoic mischievous mind monkeys.

14

Needle in a Haystack

"Hello, can you please tell me, do you have any listing of a telephone number for a library in Holborn?" I asked the telephone operator.

"You mean the British Library?" she asked. "I only have a telephone listing for a library in Holborn that's part of the British Library."

"Oh! Oh?" I nearly dropped the phone. Not only was there a library in Holborn, but it was one of the most prestigious libraries in Britain!

I took the address from the operator and drove there early one Saturday morning in February. On walking into the reception, I half expected to be laughed out of the building. I didn't have a clue about what qualifications you needed to be an admiral in the French Navy, and the combination of naval duties and higher mathematics seemed odd, even improbable. If the whole thing struck me as dubious, what would a stranger think of it?

Nevertheless, once inside the library, I went to the reception desk attended by a scruffy matronly woman. What would she be likely to know about French admirals and mathematics? I caught myself mentally and judgementally assassinating her.

"You judge a book by its cover at your own peril," Swami Shivananda had scolded me in India. "You have to look beneath the surface to discover diamonds. It's no different with people." I let go of my arrogance before speaking to the receptionist.

Tongue-tied, I squirmed inwardly as I tried to convey the gist of the message my Inner Diamond had given to me in my meditation, to look for information about 'a French admiral who had something to do with mathematics and had a name beginning with J.' I can't remember a time when I felt more like an airhead dingbat! After all, I might as well have been asking for some blindingly good book I had read in the early 80s: "I don't remember its title, but it had a red cover!"

"Mathematics, you say? You need the Euston Road site," she replied, cottoning on to just the one word she recognised. "We've relocated several sections there now, including maths and science. It's just ten minutes away." Not sure if I was being sent on a wild goose chase,

I made my way to the address the receptionist had given me. After all, except for my ego, what did I have to lose?

On arriving at the Euston Road site, I followed the signs to the reading room containing books on mathematics. I asked the Afro-Caribbean lady at the Information Desk if she could tell me how to go about finding information about a French admiral who had an interest in mathematics and whose name possibly began with the letter J.

She peered at me over the rim of her reading glasses, as if to make out whether I was one of the daily fruitcakes that walked through those library doors, or just a sad geek with nothing better to do with her life.

"Huh huh ..." she said in a laboured way, as if she had made up her mind that I was a few clowns short of a circus. Then, turning to look over her shoulder, she said, "Colin, here's another one for you!"

She might as well have announced to the library over a loudspeaker, "Hello, everyone, check out today's fruitcake in the house!" I cringed with embarrassment and just wanted to crawl under that desk of hers and hide until lights out.

A stubby man with thinning hair appeared from behind one of the tall bookshelves.

Colin glared at me through his jam-jar glasses. He seemed to be inspecting me for signs of insanity like he was used to being harassed by people asking for information about little green men in red helmets, or giant jellyfish with orange bottoms.

"How can I help you?" he asked, somewhat peevishly.

I just wanted to leg it out of the door—is there anything more humiliating than being thought of by others as ridiculous?

"This is a good time to stand firm and trust yourself, especially in the face of cynicism." I became aware of the gentle counsel of my Inner Diamond, and felt calm again. *"Trust yourself. Especially when no one else does."*

"I'm looking for information about a French admiral who was into mathematics. His name begins with a J. Can you help?" I asked confidently, calmly.

To my surprise, Colin's stance changed instantly and his face lit up and came alive like a nerd in an Apple Mac store. "Yes, I think I know who you're looking for.

A little-known interesting chap! Don't ask me for his name though. Can't remember it for the life of me."

With a spring in his step, he led me across the mezzanine and into a huge room with tall ceilings. It was as if he got a real kick from helping genuine researchers find the obscurest information.

I walked behind him, taking in the grandeur of the room. The wooden bookshelves were stacked to the ceiling with dusty old books, some leather-bound, and others that looked more modern with hardback covers. Dust particles danced in beams of light. The room was hazy, timeless. Despite trying to walk carefully, my every step sounded thunderous. What I really wanted to do was run across the floor, because the suspense and excitement were unbearable, and I could hardly contain myself. I yearned to browse the shelves—to touch and savour the sensation of holding these rare volumes in my hands.

"You'll have to climb up that ladder there," Colin said, pointing to the second row. "That's where the J section of old mathematics starts."

He then gave me a nod and turned to go. I was alone now, and nervous with anticipation. I was so close to solving the enigma. Who was this admiral? The question ran like a loop in my mind. At the same time, the monkeys had come fully alive, jibing at me so loudly that I looked around to see if anyone else could hear them: What the hell do you think you're doing here? You don't even know what you're looking for. You're just a girl with an overactive imagination. You're going to feel so foolish when you get up that ladder. And then what? How are you going to find this fancy man of yours, this admiral, out of these hundreds of books? You don't even know what you're looking for. All you've got to work with are the musings of your so-called Inner Diamond. And if you do find this admiral, how will you know he's the right one?

I climbed the wooden stepladder rung by rung and it creaked loudly like the floors, shattering a perfect pin-drop silence. I was sure that any second now, Colin was going to come back and give me my marching orders for disturbing the peace.

The climb was short, but felt like it lasted forever. I could hear my heart pounding, and wondered if the other readers in the room, or the librarians beyond, could hear it too. Lined up in front of me was row upon row of books on mathematics. Where to begin? Everything I knew about mathematics could fit on a grain of rice. I paused for a few moments, wondering how to find my personal needle in this impersonal haystack.

I noticed that my mind monkeys were less agitated now and I heard a little whisper. It was my Inner Diamond. *"Just let your hand do the choosing."*

I did exactly that and let my hand scan the hardback volumes of old books, some bound in leather, others in cotton or linen dyed in red, navy, bottle green, or black. My hand scanned the spines, at first without any preference, but then I felt my hand compelled to pull out a somewhat dusty book covered in dark blue cotton, embossed with gold letters.

I tried to focus, but the letters on the cover seemed as if they were dancing in front of my eyes.

"What the hell ...?" I opened the book at random.

I looked at the two pages now open in front of me and saw the words: Biography of Xavier Pierre Philippe Darneau de Jourdain. And there he was—an old-style etched portrait of him dressed in his naval garb. Intrigued, I read on and discovered that Xavier de Jourdain had been a naval officer who had reached the high rank of Vice Admiral in the French Navy in the nineteenth century. He was passionately interested in mathematical research and had become a pupil of one of the prominent mathematicians of the time, Michel Floreal Chasles, who was working on a treatise on geometry.

Jourdain continued his naval duties, voyaging to Indo-China and other remote places, but he utilised his spare time to solve the mathematical problems presented by Chasles. He went on to study all kinds of geometry, discovering new solutions to geometric problems, and developing the work of earlier mathematicians.

I was beyond amazed. I was stunned. My Inner Diamond had taken me so far on my journey of discovery. Its instructions had been accurate. Its guidance unerring. I had begun this search confused and more than a little sceptical, but it had led me to the exact person I'd sought. After all, there couldn't have been too many admirals in the French Navy who rose to such heights in the specific field of geometry.

But what did all this have to do with me and my *mandalas*? How was this man, long dead, relevant to me or my life?

15

Soul Centring

Dazzled by the events of earlier that day, I went home and wasted no time looking for the Chris Griscom book that Robert had brought over some months ago.

Since I had moved into this new apartment, my time had become absorbed by my job, and my evenings and weekends by painting *mandalas*. They just seemed to take on a life of their own and, one after another, they kept pouring through me. My treasure trove of books and my life's belongings were lying around in a dozen or so large cardboard boxes, piled high in my spare bedroom. The book that Robert had given me was also in one of those boxes. Somewhere.

Which one of these boxes should I begin to look in for the Chris Griscom book? I felt overwhelmed, wishing I hadn't procrastinated all these months to get better organised. I fumbled through the boxes I could get to, peeking through the slits between the flaps of the boxes that I could easily reach. As I tugged at one box, two that were piled higher up came crashing down, almost hitting my head, and nearly burying me under the books and clothes that fell out of them.

Just then, right there, as if it had fallen out of the sky, the corner of a paperback peeped out, almost buried under a mountain of sweatshirts.

I pulled it out and there was the exact book I'd been looking for! *Ecstasy is a New Frequency*. It was as if an invisible angel had somehow pulled it out of the boxes and dropped it there.

I couldn't open the book quickly enough and, sure as the guiding words of my Inner Diamond the evening before, at the back of the book on the penultimate page was the address of where Chris Griscom was based, in New Mexico.

And a contact telephone number too!

I hadn't even read this book, much less understood what she actually did.

Nonetheless, excited at the series of synchronicities and my Inner Diamond's guidance proving to be much more than just a fancy figment of my imagination, I called the phone number in the book and asked the woman who answered, "Hello, can you please tell me, is Chris doing anything on the 1st of April?"

"Why, yes!" a chirpy sounding woman answered in an American drawl. "She's scheduled to start a workshop then."

"Oh, great! What's the workshop about?" I asked, amazed at the accuracy of the information that I had been given by my Inner Diamond in last night's meditation.

"It's called 'Soul Centring' ..." As she replied, my head filled with a sudden surge of excitement at these inexplicable concurrences, that felt truly magical, and the rest of what she said was a haze.

Chris was starting a workshop on exactly the day my diamond had said. The logical next question would have been to find out what exactly 'soul centring' meant and how Chris planned to conduct the workshop and deliver its result. But it really didn't matter. My Diamond had been spot on and, what's more, I had been able to talk to and hear it, as if I had been talking to my most intimate friend. This was a big breakthrough for me, and I felt exhilarated by this exceptional experience.

"Wonderful. I'll be there." I could barely contain myself.

"Well, hang on, sweetie. We don't have enough people yet for a workshop. We'll let you know when we have enough of a number to be able to go ahead with it."

"Don't worry, it'll go ahead," I said, knowing that my Inner Diamond would not otherwise have told me to be there.

16

Completion of a Lifetime

First, I landed at the airport in Albuquerque, then travelled to my hotel in Santa Fe, which involved a long drive in the heat of New Mexico's afternoon sun. Chris's staff had arranged for me to share my hotel room with a ginger-haired, Gaelic-looking girl from San Francisco. My roommate and I decided to go in her car to where Chris conducted her sessions, in a place some miles outside of Santa Fe. Galisteo was a little village with unpaved, dusty desert paths, just off the highway.

As soon as we turned into the alley that led into this village, I thought I'd been transported back into my grandmother's tiny Gujarati village in India. The houses were sand-like baked structures, made from adobe. Old wooden logs holding up electricity wires ran all along the highway and fed these modest-looking accommodations. I wondered if there would be electric lights in these little alleys at night. Could I really be in America? How could the mighty, high tech U.S. of A look just like a little village in India? Galisteo was thoroughly charming and I fell in love with it.

After a short wait, Chris came out to greet us with her sunny blonde hair, left open and long down to the small of her back. A plain, flowing white silk dress enhanced her petite physique in an endearing way. Against the backdrop of a sheer blue cloudless sky, lit blindingly by the unblemished desert sun of New Mexico, she was the closest thing that I had ever seen resemble an angel in a human body. She had something authentic about her, fragile yet strong, and I couldn't help being drawn to her. She exuded the magnetic charisma of a person who strived to live life being true to the highest within her.

We had herbal teas while we waited for some more workshop participants to arrive, after which Chris addressed us as a group. In her introduction, she explained how the next four days would go, and also talked about the impact that clearing the residues from our past would have in our futures. I still hadn't the faintest idea how she intended to bring about such an exceptional clearing, and I was keen to get started. Shortly after Chris's talk, we were assigned to a facilitator who had been carefully chosen and trained by Chris to conduct these clearing sessions. The facilitators came and introduced themselves to whomever they were going to be working with during this workshop.

"Hi Smita, I'm Ronaldo, and will be working with you in your one-to-one sessions," a young, slightly tanned, Latin American man said, sporting a curly mop of hair. Secretly, I felt disappointed, as he looked too young to possibly conduct work of this calibre. The rooms in which the sessions were to take place were made up with minimalistic decor: white-washed walls with a dark wooden table to hold a water pitcher, some glasses, a box of tissues, and a few soft blankets and towels. A small settee had been placed in one of the corners. The massage table at the centre of room, which was floodlit with the brightness of the New Mexican sunshine, suggested that these clearing sessions required me to lie down. Ronaldo explained to me how the session would go.

"My role is to facilitate you going into the *Akashic* Records. Do you know what they are?" he asked.

"I've heard the name ..." I said, trying hard to remember where I had heard it. "Well, I know that in Sanskrit, *akash* means sky or space ... are you talking about something like that?"

"Yes, very close ..."

"Ah, I think I remember ... isn't that the library in the sky?"

"Yes, that's pretty much it." Ronaldo nodded. Before he could give me his explanation, my memory came flooding back.

"I remember now! One of the *gurus* that I met in India described them as a record of all knowledge, of all human experience, and the history of the cosmos."

"Exactly. Think of it as the 'cosmic library'." Ronaldo looked impressed that I had heard of this esoteric phenomenon. "This is where your higher Self will take you to access experiences from your past that are still hampering your life at this time. You just have to observe what you are being shown, and tell me exactly what you see and feel in that experience. At times, I will ask you the questions relevant to finding out what, from that time and experience, has left a residue that needs to be cleared. I will not speak, except to ask you specific questions and to ensure that you don't get stuck while you're viewing an old experience. Sometimes, when the memory that comes up is so intense or traumatic, a person may relive it in the present. The idea is to release the residue left by that experience, by bringing peace to it so that it loses its influence over you, and clears from driving you in the present, in your relationships or other areas of your life.

"How long will the session take?" I asked, still none the wiser about what this session was about.

"It could be one and a half hours, or two, and sometimes longer, depending on what experiences you are clearing and how you respond to accessing those memories."

I was thoroughly intrigued and fascinated by the mystery of what was about to happen. Not knowing much about how one could access the *Akashic* Records and where my Inner Diamond was going to take me, I was almost shaking with anticipation and excitement. I laid down on the comfortable massage table and closed my eyes.

Ronaldo said, "I'm first going to give you a very gentle cranial massage. It will help to relax and prepare you for this session."

He stood behind the massage table, and took my head into both his hands. I could barely feel anything at first, but then became more aware of Ronaldo's fingertips ever so gently massaging my skull. As I settled into this subtle cranial massage, even though he wasn't applying any pressure to my head, I felt Ronaldo's fingertips reaching deeper and deeper into my brain, as if somehow they were going right into different parts of my mind, bringing them alive, just like switching on lightbulbs. I was in heaven! I relaxed and almost fell asleep. My jet lag dissipated, and energy began to flow once again through my body. I lost track of time.

When Ronaldo took his hands away from my head, he said, "Are you ready to start the session now?" I nodded, though I could have done with another hour of that wonderful massage.

"Good. We're going to begin now by opening the points that are called the 'Windows to the Sky'. These points, when opened, will let you access the exact *Akashic* Record that your higher Self wants you to know about." He explained to me the next part of Chris's process that I would have to follow.

17

Symbol of Terror

Ronaldo placed the tip of his index finger on certain points on my body, starting from the centre of my chest to the head.

"Imagine that where I'm placing my finger, you are letting a beam of light pour into that point. Imagine the light is opening that point in your body and activating it," Ronaldo said.

Sceptical at first, I was astonished to find that simply visualising light enter these specific points triggered my inner vision to open up almost instantly.

"Now, I want you to ask your inner Self to take form. Ask it to take the form of a person, someone that you can easily relate to, and tell me what you are seeing as soon as you see something," he said.

A vision came into focus. I described it all to Ronaldo so that he could follow what I was seeing, where I was going, and what I was feeling.

With my eyes closed, I saw a beautiful, elegant woman with long dark hair and a honeydew complexion. She walked towards me, and stepped gracefully on the lush grass of a stunning garden bursting with flowers. She wore a long, shimmering gown in shades of lilac and purple. As she approached, the bright glow of her energy pierced through me, penetrating layers of my mind to the subtler layers of my consciousness. She came closer and took hold of my hand, and the chitter-chatter of my monkey mind fell silent. Her kind smile beamed into my heart, making me feel peaceful.

Ronaldo's voice broke into my awareness, as if he were travelling with me across time and space. "Can you tell what era you're in or which part of the world?"

But I couldn't—at least I couldn't be sure. I looked at the beautiful woman next to me, my higher Self, who would travel with me on the journey I was about to undertake. She beckoned me to look outside the small window that was closest to the entrance door of this room. A board hung just outside, suspended from a wooden bar attached to the outer wall. It had the face of a woman, wearing a black bonnet studded with large pearls, painted on it. Above, were the words 'Queen Marye Inn'.

"It looks like we're in England, in the late Middle Ages," I whispered.

I could clearly make out the sounds of people below the room I was in. In this little chamber, a thin dark-skinned woman stirred a wide cauldron on a small stove. A little girl, about seven years old, with a pleasing, roundish face, pretty brown eyes and straggly, tawny, shoulder-length hair, knelt on the floor, leant over a large wooden slate, completely absorbed in the bright, bold drawing before her.

I looked around and saw three other drawings that she must have made.

"Her drawings are exactly like the paintings that I have been making over the last year in London!" I gasped, as butterflies fluttered with excitement in my belly.

The geometric shapes had distinct, unique combinations of sharp, stunning and vibrant colours. This little girl was making *mandalas*! My higher Self took my left hand and we walked to the girl. I placed my right hand on her head and, in that instant, all normal boundaries or sensation of separateness melted. I had the powerful impression that although we had been separated by time and space, somehow she and I were one. She was a previous me and I was a future her.

We were one and the same!

As soon as I realised this, it was as if I became the little girl and could see through her eyes.

"Ma, those children are playing in the square! I want to go and play with them outside," I said in the voice of the seven-year-old.

I ran over to the small window at the back of the room and peered out, watching the children down below, wishing I could play with them. Without even looking at me, my mother answered my unspoken question. "You know they won't let you play with them." She continued stirring the cauldron with a thick ladle.

"You always tell me that, Ma." I pouted, feeling hurt.

"Oh, my love. It's for your own good. They'll only taunt you and be horrible to you."

"Why? I don't understand! Why are they horrid to me? Why don't they like me?" I asked, utterly disappointed and dejected.

"It's the way of the world, my child. They don't want you because you don't have a Pa and they think that we are witches."

"What are witches, Ma?"

"They're bad people who use spells to make bad things happen to people," she said, still stirring.

I still don't understand. "I don't do bad things to people, and nor do you. Do you, Ma? Why do they think that we're bad people?"

"It's because folk live in ignorance, my child. The Good Lord will bring about a day when folk will see the truth, not their prejudices." Mother sighed, worn down by the cruelty of folk around her.

My higher Self looked at me and whispered, "She is a seer, but she has no inkling of how visionary her words are. You are also gifted and people around here are terrified of anyone with extra-sensory powers that they themselves don't have."

I carried on staring out of the window. I couldn't help giggling to myself from time to time as I looked through the window at the four boys playing in the courtyard square below. They flicked marbles at a target and the winner was the one whose marble hit the target the most.

I played with them anyway, while Ma wasn't looking. I just had to look at the marbles and decide where I wanted them to go and they moved, as if by magic. This was so much fun! And I couldn't help giggling when the boys' marbles went off in all different directions.

Confused, one of the little boys outside in the courtyard suddenly looked up at the window and saw me staring down at him, giggling. He stopped playing and tugged at the sleeve of one of his playmates. Then he pointed up at me. All the boys stopped playing and looked up at me. The boy ran off, down an alley off the square, shouting, "Pa, Pa, Pa."

It's so much fun to play with them!

"Stop that!" Ma snapped. "It's because you do things like that that they think we're witches. You mustn't show your power to anyone, otherwise they'll kill you! Do you hear me? They'll kill us both! They don't understand that it's natural to all of us, but that some of us have it stronger than others. It makes them afraid, child. Afraid enough to want to do harm. Now don't ever do that again, and come here and have your supper."

"But I can't help it, Ma." I'd been a bad girl. I felt all mixed up. Afraid.

"You can use it, but discreetly. And remember, it's only ever to be used to do good for people, not for stupid games like marbles."

Disappointment written all over my face, shoulders slumped, I walked over to my mother and sat down on a little rug on the floor to have a supper of hot broth. After I finished eating, my mother, putting a knitted shawl around her shoulders, said, "I'm going downstairs to the inn to cook. I'll be back in an hour or so. I don't want you to open the door to anyone, to anyone at all, unless it's me. Do you understand, child? Now, bolt the door from the inside."

I nodded and did as my mother had told me to. Once I'd bolted the door after mother, I went over to a pile of slates covered in my older drawings, and scattered them all over the floor so I could find one that I hadn't yet finished.

There it was! A drawing with a big black circle at its centre. Curved orange-like slices spiralled out from the blackness to frame this dark centre. Several layers of circles that became bigger and bolder with each layer, as though emanating darkness into infinity, extended outward from the sphere formed by these slices.

My higher Self touched my forehead and I had a sudden flash. "It's the Symbol of Terror! It's the exact same one that's been haunting me and that I haven't been able to complete at home in London." Fear filled me all over again.

Then, outside, I heard loud, thumping noises. It sounded like an angry mob of men stomping up the stairs. "Open this door, or we'll break it down," a big, nasty voice boomed from the other side.

My little hands trembled. The wooden slate fell from my lap. Ma said not to open the door to anyone. I mustn't open the door ...

"Open this door!"

The door burst open and big, ugly men barged in. "There she is! Get her!"

I was scared and didn't answer. Two men stood there, holding a large heavy-looking wooden rod. One was a tall and bulky man with a rough-looking dark beard. The second man was thinner and a little shorter, and clean-shaven. They stormed into the room and saw me, kneeling on the floor, paintbrush in hand, frozen.

"So it's you! You're the one! And what's this?" One of them picked up a painting from the floor. Then another, and a third and a fourth, his face got puffier and redder, and he pointed to them so that the second man could look. "Devil's work! This is nothing less than the devil's work," the second said, working up a rage.

"It's not just the mother then. It's the child as well. You're a devil child doing the devil's work! Do you hear that?" The bigger man grabbed me by scrunching the collar of my dress, then lifted me off the floor. His oversized hand wrapped my throat and chin.

Petrified, terrorised, my eyes bulged out, as I struggled to get out of the man's grip. I shook my legs and feet so hard that, within a few moments, he had to lower me to the ground and let me loose. As soon as he put me down, I made a dash away from him, and towards the open broken door, screaming at the top of my lungs, "Ma, Ma, Ma ... " But one of the men ran and grabbed me from behind.

"Give me the rope and the sack," he said to the other man. "Give me the rope and sack, and close that door!" He took the rope and tied my hands in front of me. Then he roped my feet together to stop my frantic struggles to get away. He got out his handkerchief and stuffed it in my mouth, tying its ends at the back of my head, and then he stuffed me into the sack.

"Wait, I want that mother of hers to be lynched too. We'll get her when she's back," the tougher looking man said.

"Aye, these two are going straight to the gallows. The gibbet's the last thing they'll see."

Panic overwhelmed me.

Ronaldo's voice broke through into the room, across the divide of time and space. "What's happening to the little girl now?"

I had forgotten he was still there. His voice reminded me that I was still in the session in Galisteo. Reminded me who I actually was. I calmed a little and tried to share what was happening.

"Now the mother's walking in, and the larger, tougher man is standing hiding behind the damaged door." I relayed the scene to Ronaldo, both as an observer and also feeling the trauma for myself, as if it was still happening, to me, in this moment.

"As soon as the mother sets foot behind the threshold, he grabs her from behind the door and covers her mouth with his large hand. She's stunned, in shock. The other man's coming over. Now he's tying her mother's hands too! He's gagging her with a dirty rag lying around by her stove. Now he's going over to the sack in which the little girl is still stuffed and lets her out. The little girl's petrified. She's looking at her mother, as if to say, 'Where were you? Do something!' She's not able to breathe with her mouth still gagged." My breath, while I lay on the massage table in Galisteo, became more and more shallow as I simultaneously witnessed and experienced being at the centre of this scene, centuries apart. I fell silent as I went through the eye of the needle of this excruciating experience.

"Where are you now, Smita? Tell me what's happening now?" Ronaldo's voice felt intrusive as I was absorbed—one with what I was seeing with my inner eyes. I didn't answer and he repeated the questions.

I told him what I could see. "The bigger man's now thrown the little girl across his shoulders. The thinner man's pulling the little girl's mother, whose hands are also tied up. He's pulling her with one of his hands. With his other hand, he's waving about a bunch of the little girl's paintings, flashing them around as proof of their crime." My face stung from the tears streaming down it. Ronaldo again asked me to stay with the scene.

"They're taking the mother and the little girl outside, shouting, 'Devil child! Devil woman!' and they're parading us through the streets. People are behind us in a procession. We're all going towards an alley at the back of the square, the people of the village are marching, and shouting the chant ,'Devil child! Devil woman!'... now we're emerging into another open area, another sort of a square ... there's a tall post ....with a pike jutting out at the top of it ... the bigger man's yelling, 'Come and see it! The devil woman is going to hang on the gibbet! Come and see! We've got the devil child!' I feel so powerless! I feel helpless. Ma's struggling with the man who's pulling her behind him like an animal." I pause to catch my breath, and then carry on telling Ronaldo what's going on.

"Now they're dragging Ma to the noose ....my heart's pounding ... I'm scared ... they're putting it around her neck ... I can't bear this! They're making me watch my Ma with a noose around her neck ... Ma's gone silent ... she's just looking at me ... her eyes are red and wet ... I can't watch ... I shut my eyes tight ... I can't bear to see Ma like that. My whole body is in terror with panic. People are shouting, as if it's a chant, 'Hang the devil woman! Hang the devil child! Hang the devil woman! Hang the devil child!'"

Then I fell silent.

"What's happening now, Smita?" Ronaldo's voice broke through again. I couldn't speak. My voice was gone.

Within my mind's eye, a deathly silence now filled the square. I opened my eyes. My Ma hung by the neck, already strangled by the rope. She just dangled there, her head leaning close to her shoulder. Lifeless.

"What's happening now, Smita? Stay with me, tell me what's happening." Ronaldo's voice reached me as if from a vast distance. "Speak to me ... ," he said, trying to pull me back into communication.

"She's ... she's d—d—dead," I tell him.

"Now what's happening?" Ronaldo asked when I fell silent again.

I know I'm next. I don't want to live anymore. I want to die too. I'm ready for my death.

"Someone's picked me up ... he's taking me to the hanging post ... I have no energy ... I can't fight ... I don't want to ... Ma's gone ... I want to go with her ... I don't want to live anymore, not with these people ... I want to die." I felt lifeless.

"Keep telling me what's happening, Smita. Please don't be silent now." Urgency filled Ronaldo's voice.

"It doesn't matter anymore ... I'm next ... my heart is pounding like thunder ... they're taking Ma's dead body down ... they're putting it to one side of the gallows ... that big, ugly man who put me in the sack, he's coming over to me ... he pulls me roughly ... he gets the lynch mob chanting, 'Devil child! Devil child!' I feel black inside ... everything around me looks black too ... can't hear anything anymore ... everything's blurring in front of my eyes ... the crowd feels far away ... it all feels still and black to me ... soon I'll be with my Ma ... they're putting the noose around my neck now ... it feels hot from Ma's body ... I'm dead to their shouts and jeers ... I'm dead to everything ... the noose is tightening around my neck ... I'm choking ... this is excruciating. There's a yank as they pull the stand from beneath my feet. ... Ugh! I can't bear this!" Still speaking out loud, I moved my hands to cover my ears, in a futile attempt to block out my own voice and the sounds from within my mind.

"My neck cricks ... it's broken ... my head's hanging ... lifeless. I'm dead. They've strangled me to death! The little, poor, poor little girl ... they've killed me for no reason ... no reason at all!"

I drift off, suspended into a deep, deep, dark space.

I hear the faint sound of Ronaldo's voice speaking to me. "You're safe now. Take a few deep breaths. It's safe to breathe now."

I have nothing to say. He lets me calm down and rest for a minute or two, and then says something about colours and clearing the imprint of this experience. Eventually, I answer his questions that are the part of the process, so that we can clear this horrific experience. He asks me, "What did you carry forward from this experience?"

"I'm powerful. My power is bad. It's dangerous. It gets people killed. I'm bad because I got my mother killed. I deserve to be strangled ... it's not my mother's fault ... it's mine ... I'm sorry ... I'm so, so, so sorry, Ma. ... Will you ever forgive me?" Hot tears stream down my face.

"I must never, ever, let anyone get close to me again. It's dangerous. They'll die because of me ... I must never let anyone come close to me again ... people can't be trusted ... I will always have to be alone ... it's dangerous when someone loves me."

"Now, let's clear this some more." Ronaldo led me through some more of Chris's clearing process. Then he told me to rest as long as I needed to.

When I 'woke up', I came away from it shaken, still present to the shock and trauma that I had just relived and that had been imprinted deep within the consciousness of my soul.

I opened my eyes and Ronaldo was still sitting in the chair where I had last seen him before I went travelling into the *Akashic* Records with my Inner Diamond. "How are you feeling?" he asked. I answered with the expression in my eyes.

"You've been living all this time, blaming yourself, holding yourself responsible," he said. "That innocent, confused, traumatised little girl had made contracts with herself to not ever use her power. You had decided that your power was bad—that you were bad and dangerous. You made a contract with yourself in that time not to let anyone close to you again, because you were dangerous, because anyone who loved you could get killed," he recounted my experience. "We've cleared that now, Smita. You're free! The ramifications from this session will, starting from this moment, continue on throughout your life. This session's impact will be enormous."

The little girl's being and experience still palpated within me, even now. I, as the little girl, went to my death in the gallows with these deep, profound self-made contracts, these promises, that lived on in the depths of my soul to this point of my existence. And there was no one who could explain to the little girl otherwise.

She carried these erroneous, traumatic beliefs and self-made contracts with such conviction that they became imprinted within her, living on through time and space. I, as the little girl, had lived this experience so vividly that my soul consciousness, despite being in a different time, space and place, even in a different body, could not erase the imprints of that horrific experience.

I could now see what Chris had meant by 'residue' from past experiences. I could see how the belief of the little girl, "I deserve to be strangled because I am bad and dangerous", could have brought about being strangled by my mother as a seven-year-old even this time around. I understood now why I could not connect with people. How could I? I had made a contract with myself not to let anyone close to me, that I was dangerous for anyone who loved me—that I might cause them awful harm, maybe even death.

"Let's go outside now," Ronaldo said. "Maybe Chris is still here and you can be with her for a few moments." I felt drained. I had no energy for the moment to say or do anything. As we were walking along to the reception area, Chris came out of her little office-like room.

"How are you, Smita? How did it go?" I just looked at her. She understood. Ronaldo shared with her a summary of the session.

"Very powerful," she said. "Smita, I want you not to go anywhere at all now except straight to your hotel room. Ronaldo, are you going that way? Please could you take Smita and make sure she gets to her room safely." Then, turning to me again, she asked, "Have you had any time to buy some apple cider vinegar yet, Smita?"

I shook my head, feeling dazed.

"Ronaldo, could you please also pick up a gallon of apple cider vinegar from Fresh and Wild. Smita, when you're in your room, the only thing I want you to do is fill up the bath with warm water and pour in a couple of cups of apple cider vinegar. That's because all the residue that you've released is now hanging out in your aura. You don't want to attract more of what you've just released. The vinegar will help to clear your aura. Then, please, rest this afternoon. You'll need that to start processing all of what you've just released." Chris smiled at me with compassion.

Ronaldo dropped me off at my hotel.

18

Midday Dawn

Today, I knew the drill. I was already comfortable on the massage table, ready for my next past-life session. No sooner had Ronaldo taken me through the same steps as yesterday, to open me to the 'windows to the sky', was I into the *Akashic* Records.

"What do you see?" Ronaldo asked, poised with a pen on his notepad so that he could makes notes of whatever I recounted of my view and experience. I spoke of what I saw and the conversations that followed.

The beach heaved with life—people, people everywhere. I could see dozens of naval officers in their formal, dress uniforms from Britain, America, and France. French astronomers and specialist Oriental observers scurried about, setting up their telescopes and spectroscopes that would be essential in discerning the composition of the sun. We were all here to witness the total eclipse of the sun that was about to take place.

It seemed everyone was keenly watching the dark, overcast sky: diplomats, traders, naval officers, crews from the ships and, especially, the scientists who had come from France. All eyes were glued to the sky, hoping that the considerable expense that each nation had gone to for today's momentous event wouldn't be washed away in the tropical rains, common at this time of the year. With baited breath, we waited for the heavens to be clement and grant us cloudless skies through which the sun, the sole point of our focus, could grace us with its eclipsed presence in less than an hour from now.

"Welcome to Siam, *Capitaine* de Jourdain," a confident and jovial voice boomed from behind me, spoken in English but with a local accent. I turned around to meet the face of the voice. It was King Mongkut of Siam himself, extending royal hospitality.

On hearing my name, I remembered that Xavier Pierre Philippe Darneau de Jourdain was the mathematician who became a Vice Admiral in the French Navy and whom, a few months ago, my Inner Diamond had led me to discover in the archives of the British Library. At the time, I had been baffled as to why my Inner Diamond had taken me on the mystery tour of learning about him in the library archives but now, lying on a massage table in a remote village outside Santa Fe, New Mexico, the Diamond had led me into the *Akashic* Records to piece together the rest of this mystery.

"Thank you, your Royal Highness. We are indeed honoured to be your guests. We thank you most graciously for your generous hospitality in hosting our visit," I replied.

"The pleasure is all mine, *Capitaine*. Perhaps this is an opportunity where you will allow us to teach you Europeans about our great and ancient Eastern knowledge of science, mathematics, and astronomy!" the King said, tongue in cheek, laughing out loud and striding on, his courtiers in tow, to the British camp. No doubt, the King would then move on to the American camp to also welcome them.

Intense rivalry had arisen between the French and the Siamese King. A Pali and Sanskrit scholar, the King had studied astronomy through Siamese sources and Hindu texts, among them the ancient Indian treatise called the *Surya Siddhanta*. *Surya* was the sun, and *siddhanta* referred to principles. The King was keen to prove, in a shrewd tactical move, to avoid French domination, that the Siamese were just as advanced in certain scientific knowledge as their potential aggressors, the French and the British. Given that the Siamese King could not counter the French or British warships with his own, without spending a vast fortune in buying such war vessels and weapons from his enemies in the first place, he had decided to use intellectual tactics and a charm offensive to keep them both at bay.

The King lavished his hospitality on his precarious but important international guests. His abundant staff scuttled around offering snacks and drinks and attended to any other requests from the foreigners, or *farangs*, as they called them.

Elegantly dressed ladies strutted about, all with short, fashionable hairstyles, dressed in opulent silk

Siamese skirts, embroidered in golden and colourful silk threads. Their necks and arms were bare of jewellery, but their cummerbund-like belts studded with precious gems glinted with sparkling diamonds, rubies, emeralds, and other vibrant gems.

The King's countless horses and cattle that had been brought with him from his palace in Bangkok were busy feeding or being cleaned. Every now and then, an elephant from the King's herd could be heard trumpeting. Behind the King's wooden palace—the numerous huts and camps that had been set up on the beach—lay an impenetrable jungle, infested with mosquitoes, and which was home to wild tigers and countless monkeys. From time to time, the monkeys could be seen swinging from tree to tree and their piercing screams heard on the beach, all excited to see their private space disturbed by so much human activity. A cacophony of sounds brought an otherwise desolate beach alive with life and anticipation.

The King's men already stood at their central observation posts. Much to our vexation, in an experiment such as ours here today, even a fraction of quarter of an inch could make a big difference to our calculations, and the King had assigned us an observation post that was unlikely to give us the most accurate measurements of the eclipse—the main purpose of our astronomical efforts. However, there was little we could do about it now. He had given his own astronomers the perfect observation spot.

While I walked over to our observation post, I passed the newly erected three-storey wooden palace of King Mongkut, and saw some British naval officers emerging from the palace—heading towards their assigned observation post, no doubt. Then suddenly, there appeared a shorter man, a Siamese. He was well dressed in local attire, silken baggy culottes, and a jacket embossed with intricate embroidery and official insignia. He came dashing over to me, followed by a bevy of what appeared to be the King's ladies, some older and others no more than in their teens. The younger ladies whispered and giggled in great excitement and nudged each other.

"You must be *Capitaine* de Jourdain of the French Navy," the man said. "Forgive me for the intrusion, Sir." He introduced himself to me. He was one of the diplomats who worked in the court of King Mongkut.

"May I introduce to you their Royal Highnesses, the queens and princesses? They would very much like to speak with you, if you might be so kind as to spare them a few moments of your time." The diplomat spoke in perfect English, laden with a heavy Siamese accent.

"But of course, Sir, it would be my pleasure," I replied, also in English, though aware of my own underlying French accent. The request had surprised me somewhat, but nonetheless I felt delighted to meet the exotic royal beauties. These were the more pleasant aspects of a naval captain's duties, after all. The diplomat proceeded to introduce each of King Mongkut's queens, consorts, and princesses, of whom I counted ten in all.

"Sir, how can you know what the sun is made of if you have never been to the sun?" one asked. She had a perfectly round face, shaped eyebrows, and smooth caramel skin. I couldn't help being struck by her exceptional beauty, which her richly embroidered scarlet sarong enhanced, with its golden borders and inlaid precious gems.

"Oh! My dear lady, let me explain this to you. In fact, let me show it to you. Monsieur Hatt, is the spectrometer already set up?" I called out to Jean Jacques Hatt, the engineer-hydrographer whose attendance I had especially requested in a letter that I had sent to his superior, the director of the Paris Observatory, on the 14th of March earlier this year.

As I hailed Hatt to come over to us, a private diary that I kept in the breast pocket of my jacket fell out. I bent over to pick it up but one of the younger royal princesses got to it first. The princesses, mischievous in the naïve youthfulness of their teens, and amidst giggles galore, urged the one who held my diary in her hand to read out loud the private contents of my journal. Making polite objections, I tried to regain possession of my diary but the princess was more agile with vivacity and managed to evade my capturing it.

Amidst excited and flirtatious chuckles from her cohorts, she began to read the page on which my small notebook, embossed with the French naval seal and the French flag, had fallen open. Serendipitously, it was the draft of the letter that I had written to the director of the Paris Observatory earlier in the year. *"I still believe that Monsieur Hatt, the engineer who is the head of the astronomical and hydrographic service in Cochin China, can make useful observations of the eclipse . . . especially if a pocket or portable spectroscope were made available to him. To make good astronomical determinations, he already has the necessary instruments in his possession and the experience of this kind of observation. Due to a lack of suitable instruments, he will admittedly not be able to make photographic reproductions; but if he is, as I imagine, gifted in drawing, he will be able to supply images almost as good and exact as those."*

The young ladies were delighted to have won in their jovial mischievousness. I, meanwhile, breathed a sigh of relief that nothing of a more private or confidential nature had been divulged.

"All right, ladies, thank you," I said firmly, concealing that I could not help being somewhat charmed by this unexpected bevy of beauties—not encountering many of those on long voyages at sea—as I took hold of my notebook and replaced it in my breast pocket. I kept it with me at all times, and in it I wrote my personal and private observations, notes, and anything that could be helpful with my naval duties or in my work as a mathematician.

"Forgive my sisters for being silly and giggling so. It's just that you're so smart, *Capitaine* de Jourdain. We are not used to being surrounded by such handsome officers," one of the princesses, who looked to be more like in her twenties, said. Her striking beauty, elegant dress, and graceful gait caught my eye. If I were being honest, I could say that she struck an involuntary chord in my heart. For this I carried lifelong guilt, as I was devoted to my beloved wife.

"The pleasure is all mine, your Royal Highnesses," I said, awkwardly.

Jean-Jacques Hatt walked over from the observation post where he had been setting up his spectroscope. *"Oui, Capitaine,"* he replied. "How can I be of service to you, Sir?"

"Monsieur Hatt, these ladies would like to take a peek through your spectroscope. Is it now set up and ready?"

"Oh yes, Sir. I have just made the necessary and final adjustments." Hatt gave a slight bow.

"Very well, then. Please come over this way," I said, beckoning the royal ladies to follow me. At the observation post, they crowded around the spectroscope, shoving and pushing each other to be the first to see through it.

"Your Royal Highnesses, ladies, please form an orderly queue. Monsieur Hatt will make sure that each one of you gets to see through it. But remember, we have to be quick as the eclipse is now just minutes away," I said, injecting some discipline into their fervent enthusiasm.

With the clouds still thick in the sky, the sun remained elusive. Hatt pointed the spectroscope at a nearby flower, and invited one of the ladies at the head of the queue to come and take a look. Protocol would demand that the oldest queen would have the privilege to go first.

"This is impressive, Captain! But I only see a few coloured lines. Is that what I'm to see?"

I explained. "Indeed, your Royal Highness. When we see the light of the sun, it's made up of a whole set of colours mixed together. What the spectroscope does is to break down the light as if it were a rainbow."

"Oh! So it's a rainbow machine?" she asked, delighted by her discovery.

"Yes, ma'am, you could say that," I replied, charmed by her uncomplicated manner. "What we have found is that every element in nature has its own specific colours. So in order to know which elements are inside the sun, we simply have to look at the lines from the sun and compare them to the ones we already know from our experiments, right here on earth."

"Oh! So, does that mean that what we have here on earth is the same as what's been found on the sun?" one of the other queens asked. "Since you're so smart, *Capitaine* de Jourdain, can you please tell us what makes the sun burn so bright and so very hot?"

"Ah ha, well, that's exactly why we have come here on this expedition, to ascertain whether the flames of the sun are actually the effect of something burning, like a candle or such, or because they are something else. You see, when you just look at the sun with the naked eye, because it is so bright you cannot see that it's actually pouring out flames. So, when you have an eclipse, as we are about to have, because the sun will be obscured by the moon, which will look black, all you will see are the flames of the sun bursting out from behind the black disc of the moon. Then Monsieur Hatt, with his wonderful apparatus, will hopefully find out what the flames are made of, thereby unveiling the deep mystery of the sun, something mankind has been speculating about since the dawn of time." Suddenly, I felt excruciatingly conscious of myself as I noticed that I couldn't help myself pointing to the sky with my right index finger to stress my point, more like a professor lecturing his students than a gentleman with utterly charming ladies.

"*Capitaine* de Jourdain, the way you explain these things, you make it sound so exciting and interesting!" the beautiful princess said.

"But your Royal Highness, may I enquire, where have you learnt such good English?" I asked.

"Oh, that's all because of our wonderful governess, Mrs Anna Leonowens, who is English. She has been teaching us for a few years us at our palace in Bangkok," the noble royal said.

"That's wonderful. Is she here today?" I asked, wondering if the Princess knew that she spoke English with a Welsh accent. I can only imagine that she picked up her accent from her so-called English tutor.

"No, Sir. She has had to go to England for a few months. We hope to see her back soon," the princess said. "Now that you mention the spectroscope, I remember that sometime ago, she told us also about the discovery by an Englishman of your spectroscope. She said it used a prism to refract the different colours in the light. Oh! How I wish Mrs Anna were here today. She would be so delighted to know about your expeditions and discoveries."

How clever was this princess. She had rather impressed me.

"Take the time to get
to know your own inherent nature,
your 'svabhava'.
Then it becomes easier to
understand others."

19

Intrigues

One of the junior naval men came over and informed me that a Monsieur Stephan had asked to speak to me. I took reluctant leave of the royal ladies. "Your Highnesses, I beg leave of your good company to address pressing matters at hand." With a bow of the head, I turned and walked over to Monsieur Stephan. Out of the corner of my eye, I saw the royal party head towards the wooden palace.

"*Capitaine* de Jourdain, what a pleasure to meet you again, Sir."

I recognised the man. It was indeed Edouard Stephan, the director of the Marseilles Observatory.

"Monsieur Stephan, what a pleasure to find you here. I'm so relieved that we finally persuaded the powers that be in Paris to go ahead with this expedition so you could be here today," I said, referring to the colossal political squabbling that we had needed to go through.

"Indeed! For a long while, there was much wrangling and haggling of who should go and who should not go from France. To be honest, I had almost given up hope of seeing this eclipse altogether," Stephan replied.

"It seems this eclipse gives rise to intrigues everywhere, including in the court of the Siamese King as well as his shrewd approach towards us," I said.

"Yes, I did hear something about that, but perhaps you could enlighten me further? Since you are based in the relatively nearby Saigon, you are bound to have your finger on the pulse."

"The King wants to make sure we, the French, don't attempt to take his territories. You see, originally, the King of Siam ruled over Cambodia as well as Laos and Siam. Our taking over protection of Cambodia a few years ago from his rule has naturally generated much tension and acrimony over Laos and Siam. Of course, we would like these too—but, for now, King Mongkut holds on to his precious territories. As you see, the bay is today cluttered with enormous naval vessels: French, British, American, as well as Siamese. If ever there were to be an aggression, this would be the perfect opportunity. So he has every reason to be wary of our presence in these parts."

"Are we likely to take anymore of his territories soon?" Stephan asked.

I decided to attempt to evade a direct answer. "Let's for now concentrate on squeezing as much intellectual capital out of today's eclipse as we can, now that we have won over the politics at home and with the King."

"Surely the British are also keen to take this territory? Why else are they here?"

"Certainly they are! Let's just say that the King played his hand impressively well. I suspect the British are his guard dogs to protect him from any attempt from our side to capture Siam while we are here with our naval warships. The enemy of my enemy is my friend, so to speak."

"That is a risky yet interesting strategic manoeuvre on the King's part, but less so than not having the British here," Stephan said. "Astronomical expeditions have long been status symbols of power and imperialistic ambitions of the world's leading nations and European states, to demonstrate our scientific knowledge and power. These expeditions are as much a show of how advanced we are as an intellectual power, as they are about our cannons, steamships, and colonial presence that demonstrate how much of the world we have conquered," I said.

Then, referring to dynamics closer to home, Edouard said, "I have brought with me Monsieur Hatt, the engineer-hydrographer, at your express request. I hope that will please you, Sir."

"Very good, very good. If anyone can, I do believe that young Monsieur Hatt will be able to help us ascertain accurately what elements are emanating from the sun."

"The power struggles have been bitter, *Capitaine* de Jourdain. Deciding who should come here for this event was a battle in its own right and has set the scene for many a future intrigue." Edouard Stephan exhaled in a heavy sigh. "At one point, I feared that no one would be sent from either the Marseilles or Paris Observatories. We simply could not agree upon who should go and dilly-dallied until the eleventh hour. So fraught with delicate yet aggressive politics was this expedition, it appeared at times that advancement of science was the lesser object."

"You observe well, Monsieur Stephan. At one point, the word from Paris was that I should undertake this expedition myself, with a team of naval officers. But what good is that when all the latest equipment that we need, and the expertise to use it, resides in France at the observatories, such as yours?"

"There you have it! These expeditions have become nothing if not mired in political manoeuvrings and a stage for intellectual showmanship." The director of Marseilles Observatory gave an emphatic nod.

"And let's hope the tropical rains do not spoil the event either. We would become the laughing stock of the Parisian society!" I said, with horror at the thought.

"Yes, and of London, too," Stephan said.

"Well, now that you're here, let us make the most of it. You know the King of Siam fancies himself our equal in his knowledge," I said with amusement.

"Yes, I heard something about that. I gather he has studied from some ancient Indian texts, is that so?"

"So it seems, and this intrigued me considerably. Being in these parts, I could not resist learning about this treatise. I discovered that an English translation of the *Surya Siddhanta* had been made by an American named Ebenezer Burgess as recently as 1860. So I asked one of my American naval friends to obtain a copy for me," I told Monsieur Stephan.

"That is fascinating, indeed, Sir." Edouard Stephan spoke with genuine interest. "Please tell me more."

"The *Surya Siddhanta* is a doctrine, combining a fascinating Hindu spiritual-mystical view with mathematics and archeo-astronomy," I said. "However, it approaches the subject as somewhat of a prescription, a collection of rules that must be memorised, and then recited accurately. Providing, then, if you are able to perform the mathematical processes given in its multitude of verses, you ought to be able to work out for any given time the placement of the sun, the moon, or the five planets, and thereby predict the timings of lunar or solar eclipses."

"So, you are dependent not so much on mental acumen as memory to carry out these workings. This could make room for minute and grave error, if the tables, so to speak, are memorised or recalled imperfectly?"

"That's correct. It leaves me to conclude and concur with our scientist friend, the late Jean-Baptiste Biot, that this treatise gives results that are far from accurate," I said.

"I see. How very fascinating." Edouard rubbed his chin.

"It certainly is, Monsieur Stephan." As I agreed with him, I felt a pang of agony and angst, though for the first time, it felt strangely familiar.

I had a sudden and vivid flashback in my mind's eye.

I, de Jourdain, saw myself in an earlier time and incarnation in a sacred temple complex in north India, in the guise of a tall noble woman, when priests and priestesses were people of knowledge. They were responsible for preserving and forwarding scientific, mathematical, and mystical knowledge, largely passed down by word of mouth. Belonging to an exceptional order of priestesses, I had been taught all that was known at the time about geometry, astronomy, and astrology, as well as specific material from the mystical *Tantras* and *Vedas*. We used geometry to create beautiful symbols that were physical representations of complex multidimensional concepts and divine mystical knowledge. Among such sacred geometry were *mandalas* and *yantras*. These abstract geometric symbols were so powerful they could affect the human mind in a way that even thousands of books of hundreds of pages could not.

Me, a military man, found the image of being a woman disconcerting and difficult to digest. I battled with what I saw and experienced. These thoughts were unwelcome and uncomfortable to my rational mind and manhood, and yet it felt strangely familiar and somehow right. I had been brought up, in the Age of

Enlightenment, to make rationality the foundation of my thinking, and these thoughts were definitely irrational. They were irrational for two reasons. For one, I saw myself as a woman and not the man I prided myself to be. The other was that reincarnation wasn't part of my Christian upbringing.

I, as the Indian priestess, was utterly absorbed in observing the movement of the stars and the constitution of various constellations. I knew perfectly every line and every word of the *Surya Siddhanta* and other texts that purported to the study of the stars and planets and their impact on us. And yet, many a time my predictions were out by minutes, sometimes by as much as half a day. This frustrated me no end. At first, I imagined that it was I who had made a mistake but, later, after my female *guru* had died, I became convinced that it was the treatise that was indeed less accurate than my *gurudevi*, my female *guru*, had commanded us to believe.

Surely, this knowledge, divined directly from the Gods, must have been perfect by nature and made inaccurate only by the imperfections of the men who scribed the scriptures.

Then, in my flashback, I became an aged priestess, on my deathbed, on the temple grounds. Dissatisfied with my incomplete knowledge, I vowed to return in a future incarnation to study higher mathematics, and to continue my study of the stars, so that I may assuage my soul's thirst for learning God's secrets encoded in the mystery of the manifested universe.

This flashback brought me the realisation that perhaps my innate inclination towards mathematics, geometry, and astronomy was merely a continuation of something I had started in some previous incarnation. Perhaps it was not a coincidence that I had, in this lifetime, become a man of the seas, with much time on his hands to study geometry and algebra, to roam our planet with many an hour to kill, observing the skies from many different points on the earth.

"Our own soul
is
a piece of the stars
and it, too,
shines."

20

Eclipse

When everyone had almost given up all hope that the heavens would allow us to witness this important celestial event, quite out of the blue, the dark clouds dissipated and the sun won the day, declaring its brilliant presence.

As the British naval officer, Captain Edge, walked past our camp to his, he stopped to exchange last minute pleasantries. "Xavier, I wish you all the success with your observations, even though you do not have the benefit of our exquisite English instrumentation."

"But, *au contraire, mon ami*. It seems to me that it is you who will need some luck, as our brilliant French scientists are renowned for being the best on the planet," I said.

"We shall soon see, no doubt," the British captain said, as we thumped each other on the arm, in the spirit of camaraderie that is the hallmark of mutual respect in friendly rivalry.

I joked with him, "How provident that you should arrive by HMS Satellite, for this eclipse of the sun by the moon, the earth's satellite!"

"Providence indeed! The serendipity is all too uncanny," Edge said.

"Please, do let me know if I can be of any assistance to you, *mon ami*," I said.

"And likewise."

The appearance of the sun instantly lifted everyone's spirits. The King and his men cheered from the terrace of the palace, while I breathed relief. I had my reputation to lose had this, the most costly expedition yet to be undertaken by France, gone in vain—because it was I who had for many months campaigned vociferously in its favour. With a quick glance at my pocket watch, I noted the time to be thirty-six minutes past eleven in the morning.

Just as unexpectedly as the sun had made itself visible, did it disappear again, this time behind the dense black ball of the moon. As if in an instant, the dead of night descended. The black disc of the moon gradually moved in front of the sun, as if the sun was a round biscuit being eaten, bit by bit, until nothing was left.

Even before I had replaced my watch in the pocket of my waistcoat, the day turned pitch black, the opaque sky casting a deathly blanket of blackness over everything and everyone. People couldn't recognise even the faces of those close to them.

Womenfolk and children whimpered with terror in the suddenness of this change, and dashed for safety inside palace walls or under the cover of nearby huts. The King's elephants, horses, and cattle became still with fear in this unnatural darkness, vigilantly listening for threats. Birds landed on high branches, hiding, perching stock-still, silenced mid-tweet. The jungle fell still and silent as the dead. You could hear a feather drop, even on the grainy sands of this beach. Apart from the gentlest ebb and flow of the sea's shallow waves, just a few feet away from me, silence spread its eerie wings across the beach.

For those of us behind a telescope or spectroscope, however, these moments of silence stood sacred, as precious and historic an opportunity as we would have in our lifetimes to unveil the cosmic mystery, hitherto elusive, of the sun. Jean-Jacques Hatt, eyes glued to his spectroscope, peered intently up at the ring of brilliant, incandescent pinkish flames of sun-fire that now pierced the blackness from behind the obscured disc of the moon.

"Yoohoo, mon Capitaine!" a giggling, high-pitched voice said suddenly from behind me, in a forced accent, trying to mimic my French accent.

Once I'd recovered from the surprise, I turned around to see the beautiful princess in the red sarong standing there, her eyes glowing in the faint candlelight, and covering her excited smile with her handkerchief.

"Madame, I mean, Your Highness, what are you doing here? You should not be here, on your own, unaccompanied. Most inappropriate. May I suggest you return to the Royal Queen's party at once, before the light returns and all of this turns into an unfortunate diplomatic incident." I tried to sound stern, while my heart raced apace.

The princess caught my left arm with her right and said, *"Alléz, alléz, mon Capitaine,* quite inappropriate indeed. Don't be so stiff. Are you not happy I am here? My, don't tell me during those long boring days on your ship, you do not long for a conversation with a beautiful princess? I am pretty, am I not?" She turned and looked me straight in the eyes.

"Eh, qui, évidemment, ma chère, euh, Your Highness, I mean, *très belle,* very beautiful!" I found myself fumbling,

confusing French and English and feeling utterly disoriented.

"You see, that was not so hard, was it now, *mon Capitaine?*" she said with mischief.

"What was not hard?" I asked, horrified, still confused and feeling myself blush, my face turning red. Luckily, it remained pitch dark.

"Having a normal man and woman conversation, silly, even while wearing your beautiful uniform, Xavier. You are a bit earnest indeed, funny even!" she said, toying ruthlessly with my emotions.

"But, my Lady," I said, composing myself once again. "Please, I must implore you to go. We have only a few minutes left for our experiment." I gently removed her arm from mine and took a step back.

Just at that moment, to my relief, Hatt called out in a loud whisper in excitement.

"*Capitaine,*" Hatt's whisper landed deafening as thunder in the perfect silence. "*Capitaine,* you need to see this," he said, dejection heavy in his voice. "This is quite perplexing."

While I rushed to see what Hatt wanted to show me, the Princess started walking back to the King's side of the beach, looking over her shoulder, throwing me a kiss with her hand and whispering, "See you later, *mon Capitaine*. Don't forget about your beautiful princess."

Indeed, as it turned out, I never did forget her.

"*Mon Dieu!*" I said, peering into the spectroscope, and looking through the lines emanating from the sun. "It's hydrogen. Definitely hydrogen!"

"*Oui, oui!*" Hatt said in a hushed voice. "But hydrogen doesn't burn, and yet there are definitely fiery flares on the sun. Could it be that hydrogen does burn after all?" he said, beleaguered with disappointment that his name would not to go down in history as being the first to solve the mystery of what causes the sun to burn.

Just then, I found myself distracted by a sudden dazzle and glisten in the darkness when the corner of my eye caught a visual alchemy taking place a little further along the beach. A small camp fire had been lit, it seemed by someone in the King's party, perhaps to allay the shock and fright of the royal children or ladies of the pitch black at midday, and most definitely for roasting a feast of pig and chicken and other lavish delicacies for the King and his guests. As I turned to look, to my surprise the dazzling gleam was the reflection of the diamonds, worn by the royal ladies in their opulent waist belts, sparkling like stars.

The razzle-dazzle from the sparkling diamonds, mesmerising my attention momentarily, inspired an unexpected epiphany.

"Ah! But don't you see, this is indeed extraordinary, Lieutenant Hatt," I said, my mind awakened with awareness, just as the sun emerged slowly into daylight from behind the darkness of the moon.

"We already know from Monsieur Copernicus that the sun is a star. We now also know what is emanating in abundance from the sun is hydrogen and other elements that are common to our earth. We also know that the stars are made up of the same elements as the sun," I said, with the excitement of a little boy on his first ride on a steam engine, as I joined the dots that had not, to this point in scientific history, been connected.

"Yes, but I am not sure I am following you, *Capitaine*," Hatt said, somewhat meekly.

"Don't you see? This spectacular midday dawn gives us a quantum leap in our understanding so far.

It is now safe to deduce that our earth and, indeed, we human beings are made of the same stuff as the stars!" I reached out and grabbed Hatt by the shoulders. "This is groundbreaking, Lieutenant Hatt! *We can now be certain that we are made of the stars!* Made of star stuff, our souls shine like sparkling diamonds, such as those adorned by the royal ladies of Siam over there. That is divine, is it not, Lieutenant Hatt?" I felt overwhelmed with exhilaration, but then regained my composure, as befitted a mathematician and captain of the French Navy.

"Yes, yes! I did not put two and two together so quickly, *Capitaine* de Jourdain. This is a breakthrough in our understanding, indeed."

Although we hadn't solved the mystery of what was actually burning in and around the sun, we had found the indisputable evidence that connected us, and our planet, to the cosmic stars.

"It's true, we still don't know why there appear to be fires on the sun. I do not think, however, that the perpetual solar flares are a consequence of continual arrival of human souls going up to the sun, as asserted by our friend, the religious scientist Louis Figuer," I said with renewed conviction.

"Surely not. It surely is not souls burning inside the sun." Hatt looked horrified.

Every scientific discovery about our place in the solar system and cosmos brought more clarity that science had a role to play distinct from that of religion. Until recently, religion and science were both perceived as paths to 'know' God. The two, until now, had mingled together quite naturally. Men of religion had often also been scientists, and scientists looked for God through the study of Nature. Indeed, even the great Michael Faraday, just like Newton before him, believed in the absolute authority of the Bible and considered science as a means to shine a light on what he called 'God's other book', in other words: Nature.

"I tend to agree with your view, *Capitaine*. Perhaps one of these days, we will also discover what makes the sun burn," Hatt replied.

"Would you say it was still worth the long voyage and all the political haggling, Lieutenant Hatt?" I asked, amused.

"Indeed it was, Sir. I have never seen an eclipse so long, exactly six minutes and forty seconds," he said. "And, it is not a small thing to make conclusive that we are made of stars."

With the sun dispelling the deathly darkness of the total eclipse, which had lasted for an entire six minutes and forty seconds, an eternity to creatures that had gone into hiding, life returned anew on the beach. Birds resumed flight and chirped to their hearts' content. Monkeys, too, came back to their life of mischief, swinging from tree to tree. Elephants trumpeted louder than before, harmonising with the thundering ceremonial drums and trumpets, from the nearby village, to shock away the demon Hindu God Rahu, who, for those six minutes and forty seconds, had abducted the sun in his clutches, according to Siamese and Hindu beliefs. The King summoned the blast of music to begin while he took his purification bath to rid himself of the murky, inauspicious energies of the eclipse. Everyone celebrated with abandon.

While I watched life return to normal on the beach, I felt a sense of satisfaction and fulfilment that I had not felt so completely until now in my life. This midday dawn, conscious awareness arose in me of the deeper purpose behind the thirst that had me roaming the high seas, and avidly absorbing every mathematical construct and striving to keep up with every latest scientific development. Every eclipse held the promise of a new revelation, a new dilemma making itself known, a new mystery being unveiled.

I wanted to discover the secrets that lay in God's Book of Nature.

With the flashing reflection of the sparkling diamonds on the royal ladies' waist belts, I clearly saw that our own soul is a piece of the stars and that it, too, shines. When this luminous Inner Diamond returns incarnate in the human form time and again, just as the Hindus claim it does, as I learned from their scriptures while seafaring in South East Asia, then its spark breathes life into the human body, granting it life. When the spark leaves the body, so does it leave the body lifeless, taking the 'being' out of the 'human', returning into its radiant, essential nature.

I now knew that there was a part of us, this Inner Diamond, as I took to calling it, at the very core of each of us, of each living thing.

I wanted to know this unique, mystical phenomenon more, intimately more.

What a day it had turned out to be. In a matter of a few mere minutes, an insight as deep as the night had forever altered the course of science, and a magic encounter with an angelic princess made an unexpected dent in my own, otherwise rather predictable, personal life.

Vying to see my beautiful princess again, I asked Hatt to complete writing down the measurements of the eclipse and to restore our delicate instruments back to their boxes. I strode over, with anticipation, towards the King's beach palace, nurturing in my heart the secret hope of seeing my scarlet princess, in the light of day. Just as I arrived outside the palace, to my horror, I saw the head queen prematurely leaving with her party of royal ladies. Many of them had looks of disappointment on their faces as, just like me, they had been looking forward to the lavish party anticipated to take place that evening for the King's international guests.

The royal ladies processioned past me, my scarlet princess in the middle of the crowd. As she went by, she turned her head, looking at me from a distance, waving her handkerchief in despair, longing for eye contact. I, helpless, looked on, with sudden feelings of being happy, sad, romantic, and confused all at once, but above all noticing a pang of loneliness arising. This romance, that would forever remain unfulfilled, nothing more than the short passionate encounter with someone who, in an instant, felt like a kindred spirit, a reflection of myself. The memory would come to burn within me of this daring, somewhat rebellious, intelligent, beautiful, and effervescent princess.

I fell silent, then Ronaldo's voice brought me back into the present.

"Is there anything left incomplete for you in that lifetime?" he asked.

"Perhaps the thing is to now let go of the underlying sense of unfulfilled romantic longings that seem to be blocking me from moving on in intimate relationships. Now I can see that it's partly these this that makes me feel like a cardboard cut-out," I said, already feeling enormously relieved.

"Is there anything else you'd like to say about those two lifetimes?" Ronaldo asked.

By now, I was saturated, and could think no more.

"It seems to me that both of those lifetimes, as de Jourdain and as the priestess, were incredibly important in your soul's development," Ronaldo said. "They were the basis of your discovering the existence of the Inner Diamond. Also, in the lifetime that you saw yesterday, as the little girl in the Middle Ages who drew *mandalas* and was hung, she remembered her ancient knowledge as the priestess. Unfortunately, in the Middle Ages, such higher knowledge was deemed to be sorcery and got you killed."

21

Full Circle

It had become clear to me that the way the Inner Diamond worked was mysterious—non-linear, and not always easy to understand by the rational mind. The reason I had gone to Sante Fe was because I was stuck in the fear that had emerged from painting the Symbol of Terror. Or so I thought. Instead, I had come away with something that proved to be far, far more precious. The Symbol of Terror was inextricably linked to the woman who was my mother then and, as it turned out, in this life too, and with whom I had been put to an abrupt death in circumstances of deep turmoil and turbulence.

In those last dying moments, my emotions were loaded with terror, anguish, and feelings of abandonment. As the fanatical lynch mob dragged me through the streets, I was powerless. The only person to whom I could call out to for help was my mother. I shouted out to her incessantly, at the top of my lungs, but she could do nothing to help. She, too, was helpless. Being a mere child, I felt utterly abandoned.

"Why doesn't my Ma protect me from these bad people? I will never, ever trust her again," the thought lacerated my mind like a sharp knife through tender flesh. Traumatic feelings of never being able to trust anyone to take care of me ever again, cut a deep groove in my consciousness, creating *samskaras* (imprints stamped in the mind) which I took with me in my final, parting breath. At the same time, I also felt profound guilt: that it was because of me, because I was 'bad', because the people of this village believed that I was the 'devil child', that she had been dragged through the streets to a horrific death.

Being able to observe and re-experience those past events from within the present, from the vantage point and wisdom of my current life, I was now able to relive, as an objective witness, the experience of what had happened in that lifetime between me and my mother. Since I was viewing that past from the future, I had the advantage of applying my awareness in the present moment, awareness that was more developed than it had been in that previous lifetime. From the perspective of my present life, I was now more capable of seeing more dispassionately what had happened, not just from my own perspective but more importantly, from that of my mother, too.

This meant that I could fill in the blanks, so to speak, of those things that I had died not seeing, knowing, or comprehending. I could now see, through the medium of the Akashic, that which I had not been able to see or understand at that time, while we were in the process of being forcefully abducted and taken through the village to be lynched by the frenzied mob.

I saw that in the moment of the lynching, my mother had been inconsolable at being separated from me. She, like a struggling fish out of water, writhed and wriggled under the force of the hands of her aggressors, calling out my name incessantly, though I could not hear her in all the furore of the event. I was kept far apart from her, not being allowed to catch even just a glance of her, and so had not been able to witness her mortal distress. Through the medium of the *Akashic* Records, I was able to get a clear and objective experience of all the emotional turmoil in which both she and I had died, agonisingly and abruptly separated from each other. She parted from me and that life with a sense of profound guilt and helplessness. Meanwhile, I died with three fatal *samskaras* or impressions branded in the mind: I could never again count on her to look after me; men could not be trusted; and I vowed that, in the future, I would have to take care of my self.

Both of us died in the gallows in a turmoil of guilt, anguish, anger, and a sense of abandonment.

By accessing this lifetime through the *Akashic* Records, it became clear to me that the deep impressions which I had taken to my death, those of the seven-year-old child who took her last breath convinced that she had, in her most deadly hour of need, been abandoned by her mother, was not what had actually happened. I had now been able to witness that the mother of that little girl had died racked with guilt at not being able to protect her. Moreover, I could now better understand why she, that woman who had died in the gallows with me and who was my mother in this very lifetime, was even now suffering in her current life from feelings of that guilt and powerlessness. In the same way as I, in my subconscious mind, could not trust my mother to look after me, it seemed that my mother carried indelible imprints of guilt. Both of us were plagued by residues of anger towards each other.

We went to our death with these contradictory but potent and unresolved emotions. In the midst of shock and the deathly gravity of the situation, these emotions lingered on and, in this lifetime, completely outside of our conscious control, festered in the subconscious mind without any conscious interaction from us. These subtle yet profound imprints had me and my mother gripped by a past long gone and its physical trace erased. They had taken on a life of their own and they called the shots of how we related to each other in this lifetime. Out of our conscious awareness, however faint those memories of our souls, they ran our lives just as powerfully even now. They remained unfinished business.

Through the evidence of my current lifetime, I learnt that the *jiva-atman*, which exists in a continuum, does not recognise a new time and space. These old traumatised memories, engraved as grooves in our consciousness, continued to inform our inclinations and thoughts from the layer of the subconscious. I could see, clear as day, that the memories and decisions that my mother and I had carried forward from this one lifetime shaped our feelings towards each other in the here and now. They still impacted us, hundreds of years after that event in Queen Mary's reign. Those imprints inclined us to our love for each other but, at the same time, kept us painfully apart, like two magnets whose force field repelled each other.

A fresh, healthy, and fulfilling relationship had simply not been available between my mother and me.

Until now, that is.

Since I'd seen what had happened, during the session in Sante Fe, and how its emotional loose ends still ran through our lives and bound us together, I could finally bring closure to this terrible *karmic* turmoil, and triumph over it.

I went back home to London with a new lease of life, feeling as if I had been released from a prison sentence of lifetimes. For the first time in many years, I couldn't wait to go and see my mum. Those sessions in Santa Fe had helped me to see the truth of what had happened, and now saw both of us in a new light, through the perspective of higher awareness. Instead of feeling the bitterness of blaming my mum for not having been there for me through my childhood, and feeling wicked and guilty for distancing myself from her, a spontaneous sense of compassion and acceptance filled me. Independent of me or Papa or Motabhai, I saw my mum from a fresh context: a soul in her own right, a soul on a quest to untangle herself from the intertwined ropes that bound her to the illusions of the ego.

The very next day after coming back from Santa Fe, after having slept through my jet lag, the first thing I did was to go and see my mum. She was somewhat startled and surprised when I arrived unannounced and in the middle of a working day. Still at the front door, in the entrance of the hallway, I reached out and gave her a huge, warm hug and kissed her soft cheeks. She, still wooden in her response, didn't react with equal warmth or embrace. How could she? She would need time to adjust to the new dynamic that would be formed, releasing the energy of the old *karma* from which I had extracted us both. We would both need time to adjust and develop our bond afresh, free from ages old blame and expectation.

I sat her down at the small kitchen table and then, like a gushing waterfall, told her all about what I had just discovered in my sessions in Santa Fe, and even as I explained everything to her, I could see a relief come over her face, making her instantly look ten years younger. When I looked into her eyes, I realised that the resignation I had seen deepen in her eyes over the years was that of a soul desperately seeking for her personal soul experience to be validated, one who had given up ever being understood by another, of being 'gotten'.

"Mum, I can't imagine how much pain you must have felt when I resisted you all these years. I can see now how you must feel rejected by me, when I would rather seek comfort from others instead of coming to you. I also realised after that session in Santa Fe that having vowed never to allow you to look after me again, a part of me was punishing you for abandoning me to those awful people. The child that I was, being dragged through those streets, I really did believe that you abandoned me, that you did not protect me—but the reality was quite different when I was able to see it from a higher perspective," I said, feeling heartfelt remorse.

"Mamma, I ask you to forgive me for not letting you be my mother. Will you please forgive me?" I asked, letting drop every layer of defensiveness that I had built up towards her.

"*Pagal*," she replied, calling me a silly girl, "there's nothing to forgive! It's not your fault. Things have happened of their own accord and there's nothing for you to apologise for. If anyone should be apologising, it's me. I'm the one that's failed you, to be there when you needed me, to be the mother you deserve ..." To this day, never had I seen a tear in my mother's eyes, but now something melted in her and she welled up.

I stopped her in mid-sentence. "Mum, you haven't failed me. You couldn't help how life has unfolded for you, either. You must never apologise to me for anything. You have given me life, Mum. What can you, you who have given me the biggest gift possible, what could you possibly have to apologise for?" Now my eyes were filled with tears of love, love which had been forcefully suppressed beneath layers and layers of illusion, misunderstanding, and unresolved emotions.

"I have really missed you," my mum said, opening up. "It all makes sense now, with what you have seen about this past-life connection. Whenever you were not with me, when I was really ill, all I could think about was you, if you were okay, if you were eating enough, if you were safe. *Is she safe?* Even when you left home after you bought your own flat, I would call you every day, several times a day, because I felt restless about your well-being and safety."

"Isn't that what mothers do?" I asked, smiling.

"Yes, but this is that and much more. I have a very clear memory of the moment when, as a soul, I was ready to take birth in this lifetime. I remember seeing myself, though I was still a soul without body, as a girl of about ten years old wearing a half *sari*, sky blue in colour. I was floating around just outside the mansion of the well-known Karia family of Porbandar. They were one of the wealthiest families in Gujarat, and I was being offered a choice for my next incarnation—to take birth there, and I was also being shown two other families. There, with the Karia family, I could feel heat emanating from their mansion," Mum said.

"Why was there heat?" I asked, wanting to understand if the heat represented something symbolic.

"It was the heat of money, of wealth. But it wasn't a healthy wealth. There was something tainted about it. Intuitively, I sensed that if I had chosen to go there, I would have had a short life. I was being shown that I would have died when I was just ten," she replied.

"Maybe that's why you were seeing yourself as a little girl who was around ten years old."

"Maybe, and floating around in my soul awareness outside of that big mansion, I could sense that in taking birth there, I would step into the Karia family's *karma* and that would not have progressed my soul in the way I now needed to. Besides, I had a strong sense that I needed to bring this one little girl into the world. I could see her and feel her around me. She was a bubbly, vibrant little girl, bright and full of life. I felt very strongly that I had to give her birth." Mum had never before talked to me with so much openness and I was captivated by how lucidly she remembered everything.

"Was that me, Mum?" I asked in a tiny voice.

"Yes, I felt very strongly that I had to give birth to you," she said. "It was as if I was calling out to you even before I was born, wishing to find you again, to be with you. My soul was restless and I knew I had to bring you to life. Then, I was shown a man who was a rising star of a lawyer. I was shown that he would become one of the most respected and successful people of his generation and my soul pulled me to him. I also saw your father's soul, waiting for me. It felt right that I should choose them for experiencing my incarnation and I did. That felt so right."

"Perhaps that's because you left some significant part of your soul behind when you were killed, the last time you and I were together, in that past life I saw in Santa Fe? When they were taking you to the gallows, you were incessantly calling out my name and I could see, even in your very final breath, you called out to me. Mine was the last name you uttered with your last breath."

"That is how it must have been. It all makes sense. Do you know, in our spiritual philosophy, it is believed that whatever your last thought is in the moment you die, that thought is what will propel you into your future incarnation? That final thought in the moment of death casts the seed of what will manifest in your next life." As Mum spoke, I could see the insights making her eyes come more and more alive.

"So you were left vying for me, the little girl that you wanted to protect with all your might but could not. You died unable to fulfil your duty and you wanted another chance to bring things full circle?" I asked.

"It certainly felt like that. Only I didn't know why. Now, with what you have explained, something in my understanding has clicked into place. It makes perfect sense," Mum said with obvious relief and satisfaction.

"Would what I saw about that past life explain why you were angry with me when you did see me? Did you feel a sense of anger towards me as well as love?" I asked, trying to piece the puzzle together.

"Yes, of course. I loved you and wanted to keep you safe but then, when I did see you, something in me involuntarily wanted to shake you up! And then I felt so unbearably guilty too, but it was such an automatic reaction, that I simply couldn't stop myself in the moment," she said. I was amazed to see how lucid and clear my mum remembered the details of her life, and my heart could not help flowing over with compassion for her, for her humanity.

I felt a need to explain. "Mum, it's no wonder that you have been unable to fully be here, in this life. You left pieces of yourself, a precious part of your soul, in that village square where we were hanged."

Stunned, she looked at me, remaining silent for a few moments as what I had said clicked in her awareness. "*Haa, kherakhar! Mane avuj thaaya rakhe che.*

Tu kay che e saav saachu che. Really! That's exactly how I've been feeling. It's true that I feel as if a part of me is not here, like I'm wandering here and looking for something important there. My soul feels like it has never fully arrived in this body, in this life," my mum burst out. It was as if a light that must have dimmed a long time ago suddenly switched on within her. "You see, when you die a sudden and violent death, your soul might not be ready or able to leave that time and place fully."

"Well, Mum, it was what you call the *antar-Atman*, what I call my Inner Diamond, that prompted me to make this journey, but I thought I was going to Santa Fe for a different reason altogether. It was only after I completed my very first session there that I realised the purpose of doing those past-life sessions was to be able to retrieve any aspect of ourselves that we might have left behind, especially in circumstances of a difficult death." My mother listened intently as I spoke.

"It just goes to show that when you have purity of *bhavana*, inner state, you get given all the solutions, even to resolve difficult *karma*," Mum said.

"Yeah, it's really like that, isn't it?" I said. "Even in my meditations and prayers, I've bared my soul as authentically as I know how, that I want my life to be an expression of my soul. I've asked for the way to be cleared so that I can be the highest that I can possibly be in this lifetime," I said, not taking for granted for a moment that this conversation I was having with my mother was an exceptional one. It would set the tone of our relationship to come. Never had I been able to engage with my mother so soulfully.

"The other thing that was so amazing about these sessions was they were all about looking to see what loose ends the soul needs to tie up, especially in important relationships," I said, excited. "At the end of each session, the person guiding me through the session would ask me if there was something I needed from someone else or they needed from me, so that we could bring that cycle of our *karma* together to a close."

As she shuffled in her chair, all fired up, I realised that I had never seen my mum so alive and present as she listened to what I was telling her. Fascinated, she asked, "Really? *E to bhahuj saaru kehevaay*. That's a wonderful thing to be able to do. How do you do that?"

"Well, it's a symbolic gesture but because you're consciously addressing it with your own focused awareness, it really helps you to let go of something you might not even have realised your mind was gripping to. So the facilitator simply asked me what object or symbol the person with whom I had something unfinished could give me, so that, in their giving and my receiving it, we could close that chapter between us and move on. I would also mentally ask that person what they needed from me. We were able to bring things to a harmonious close through the gift, a symbolic object that they asked for and that I gave them. That object, such as a gold ring, symbolically represented the thing that in that lifetime they desired or expected from me, say love, or acceptance, or respect. It's that simple, but it really works," I said, all charged.

"*He? Bus? Aatluj karvaa nu? Really?* Is that all you have to do?" Mum asked, genuinely interested.

"I know, it really *is* that simple!"

"But, how would you know what thing to ask for? Or what symbol is the right one?" she asked.

"You see, you don't think about it. If you listen, it's the Inner Diamond that tells you or brings it into your mind," I said.

"Hmmm ... I see," Mum said thoughtfully, taking it all in.

"It's like an intuitive knowing. You just *know*, also from what you've witnessed and experienced in the session of that life, what was missing between you and the other person, and then what would resolve it, make it whole, if they were able to give that thing to you, even if it's symbolic. See, the important thing is that you bring it out of the back of your subconscious and into your knowing mind. Then, you see, you can put this issue to bed, this thing that you might not have been aware of but that had so much power over you anyway. So much so that it's continued to shape your relationship with that person even in the present, almost without you having control over it."

"That would explain why I wanted to be so close to you and yet every time I tried, I would do or say something to drive you away even further," Mum said, still deep in thought, regret coming over her face.

"Right, exactly. And that's how I felt. I couldn't wait to see you. Like that time when you came back from the hospital, when we were still in Porbandar, I was so, so excited. I couldn't eat and I kept Motabhai up all night with my twittering about what we could do together when you were finally home. All the things that I'd been dreaming about doing with you. But when you were finally in front of me, I just wanted to run away. And I've hated myself ever since for doing that to you," I said, buried remorse shooting to the surface. "I'm so, so sorry, Mum. I didn't mean to do that, but I just couldn't help myself and, what's worse, it seemed like I didn't have control over what my heart wanted to do and what my mind made me do. It's been tearing me apart!" I could feel the pain of these contradictions, etched on my face. "I wish I could turn back the clock and do it all over again, Mum." I put my arms around her once again.

"It's okay, *beta*. I also wish I had been able to do things differently. It's okay. I wouldn't change you for the world," she said with tenderness, and her big-hearted forgiveness drew me closer to her. Perhaps for the first time, I was able to really see what a sweet, kind soul my mother was. Wanting to understand more, she asked, "What else happened, once you exchanged the gifts with each other?"

"Well, in just shining the light of the Self's awareness on the situation in that particular aspect of my past life, I was able to symbolically recover pieces of not just myself that I had left behind, but I was able to do the same for you. So not only did I close the chapter of that awful lifetime for myself but also for you. Mamma, I'm absolutely sure, that you will begin to feel more 'together' and more at peace because of this."

I paused, and in the silence as my words sunk in, she looked thoughtfully into a corner of her kitchen, and then said, "I have never felt worthy of being your mother.

No matter how much I tried not to, I could not help it—I just yearned and yearned to be close to you ... even when I was so ill, when we were still in India, do you know that I used to sneak out from the room at Granddad Motabhai's where I was supposed to stay all day long, hoping to find you at your grandmother Motima's house? I used to sneak out just to get a glimpse of you. But whenever I came around, I would find the doors and windows locked with no one there. Not being able to see you was like crawling through the desert, parched, in search of a few drops of water, a glimpse of your face."

"Oh, Mum! I had no idea how awful that must have been for you. I'm *so* sorry." My stomach twisted into knots. It was as if I felt, all at once, the pain and torture she must have suffered all those years.

"It feels right, everything you've just told me," she said. "It makes complete sense, and just in your sharing all this, something in me has settled down, that restlessness that I have had within me for so long, it's suddenly disappeared. I'm feeling so much at peace." She looked at me, vulnerability in her eyes, and said, "Thank you, *beta*."

I had never seen her look at me this way before in this lifetime. She had a warm, tender, loving smile on her face, her eyes glowing with happiness, while tears streamed down her face. She came close to me again and put one hand gently on my face and another around my waist. "May you always be healthy and happy, *beta*. May God always keep you protected from harm and fulfil all your heart's desires."

These blessings meant the world to me, coming from this sensitive, loving soul whom, I now realised, it was a privilege to have as my mother. How she had shaped my life! Who else, but someone who loved me more than life itself, could bear such difficulties so that my soul's light could shine brighter?

As I looked at her, not able to stop my tears, it occurred to me that words were inadequate to explain how much satisfaction and fulfilment filled me in this moment. Through doing this work, I had been fulfilling my life's purpose, I realised. The work I had done in those sessions in Santa Fe was nothing less than a part of the *dharma* or *karmic* duty that I had committed to undertake in this life.

This release from *karmic* bondage was what I called 'moksha now'—jivan-mukti—or liberation of the soul: in action, while fully alive.

I embraced my mother as if for the first time. My heart went out to this soul who had been playing the difficult role of being a mother, my mother. Both of us wept a long time in each other's arms, letting the tears flow their natural course, unravelling age-old sorrow and regret until no more such tears remained. The river of our tears brought about a new lease of life and, above all, acceptance and peace.

Beneath the sadness of our journey together, were buried the seeds of unconditional love. Love that would triumph and, in due course, I was certain would give birth to green shoots of a joyful and fulfilling relationship with my beloved mother, to enjoy in the golden years of her life.

22

The Digital Monk

Several years had passed since I visited Santa Fe and uncovered past lives from which flowed threads of *karma* that still entwined with my current life.

I now found myself in the ancient Indian town of Rishikesh once again, in the foothills of the Himalayas, right in the magical spot where the sacred river known as Mother Ganga or Ganges emerges from the mountain valleys and bursts onto the great Indian Plains. I went into the treasure trove of a bookshop called the Ganga Bookstore, an appropriate name, since it was directly on the banks of the River Ganga. The shop was laden, floor to ceiling, often with double and triple rows of books lining the crammed bookshelves. Piles of books were stacked everywhere on the floor, so that you could barely move around.

All kinds of contemporary and ancient books could be found here, on subjects ranging from ancient mathematics to astronomy, to Vedic astrology to *tantrik* yoga of the Middle Ages, to biographies of saints and holy people. Whenever I had walked into such bookshops in

India on previous trips, I had always found unusual or rare books to delight the mind and that were no longer in print. Though I had no idea what I was looking for, I hoped to stumble across little-known books on fascinating subjects. The driver who'd accompanied me to the world-renowned Parmarth Niketan Ashram on the Ganges riverbank, said that I would not be disappointed with the Ganga Bookstore. He said that it was not far from Lakshman Jhula, where we would have to cross the River Ganges to get to the *ashram*.

Once at the *ashram*, it was my intention to meet with a *swami* whose smiling face I had seen in a dream some months before coming to Rishikesh, though I did not then know who he was. The day after that dream, I went as usual to drop off some groceries at my mother's. Right there, on her living room table, was the well-known monthly British-Gujarati magazine, *Garvi Gujarat*. She had just received it that day and, from its front page, a photo of this very same swami stared up at me. His name, I learnt, was Pujya Swami Chidanand Saraswati, who my mum said was known across India simply as 'Muniji'. Parmarth Niketan was his *ashram*. Something about this synchronicity had pulled me to return to Rishikesh, some ten years after a trip on which I had assisted Swami Shivananda there at the medical eye camp.

As it happened, I would develop a special relationship with Muniji over time, but there was something else too that seemed to have called me to Rishikesh.

"You must have a bigger than average interest in Indian astrology if you're interested in books about divisional *varga* charts and *dasha* time periods?" A man with a beard, in white renunciate's garb, stood behind me. His eyes twinkled as he smiled. He helped me with the pile of little-known esoteric books, mostly on technicalities of Indian astrology and old mathematics, in my arms, as I struggled to not drop them all on the floor.

Yes, Sherlock, I thought, but smiled and said, "That's true. I do have a bit of a fascination with it." I was polite but somewhat cynical, as I walked towards the cashier to pay for my purchases. I'd come across many such renunciates, *sadhus*, and so-called *swamis*, much like this man, and was less than impressed with most, least of all where knowledge of Indian astrology was concerned. Most, according to me, were superstitious flake-heads. The few I had met just did not have the breadth and depth of knowledge of this vast science. Most were plain-and-simple lazy, not bothering to do the homework to do justice to reading a birth chart in depth enough to make any real difference.

The man in the white garb left as I waited for the owner to finish putting my books in a bag. I still had another couple of hours to kill before heading to the *ashram* and I was eager to dive into one of the books I had just bought. Immediately outside the bookshop, facing the Ganges, was the German Bakery. I looked around for somewhere to sit but the place was heaving, full of Western and Indian tourists alike. A waiter took me to the only seat that was available on the balcony, overlooking the holy river, and it was right next to the white-robed man I had just spoken to in the shop. He nodded and smiled at me. When I noticed that he was busy flicking through the screen of his Blackberry, while powering up his latest Windows computer, I couldn't help smiling to myself.

"Would you mind if I take a picture of you?" I asked, grinning.

"Er, sure. But why do you want a picture of *me*?" he asked, puzzled. He spoke with an accent that sounded much like that of my colleagues from Bangalore, in the south.

"Because you're the icon of the Digital Monk," I replied, laughing. "The perfect anachronism."

He laughed and I took a snap of the laughing Digital Monk.

"Why do you need a computer?" I asked, cheekily. "Aren't you supposed to be all white robes and sandals, and renounce the evil of all things material?"

The Digital Monk laughed again. "Oh, because I write a lot and there's all kinds of software on there, including a superb astrology software that I like to use from time to time," he replied. "It's a fascination of mine, too."

"That's why you recognised the books I just bought," I said. The waiter came over and hovered about for our order. The white-robed man seemed to have something genuine about him and the air of someone learned.

"I'll have an English breakfast tea with slices of lemon. How about you?" I said, turning to the monk.

He glanced through the German Bakery's extensive menu and replied, "I'll have a yak cheese sandwich."

A yak cheese sandwich! Was that a joke? I scanned the menu. Sure enough, a caprese sandwich of yak cheese seemed to be something of a speciality at the German Bakery.

"Oh, they call me Balanand Baba," he introduced himself.

"Hi, I'm Smita. Pleased to meet you."

"Where are you from?" he asked.

I told him that I was from London and he asked me a few more questions about my trip to India.

"Are you based in Rishikesh? Have you always been a renunciate?" I asked.

"Oh no, I used to be a computer engineer. I worked for thirty-five years in banks and information technology companies and, now that my dear wife has passed away and I have no children, I have devoted my life to serving God," he said. "I'm here for some social work in Rishikesh with some fellow renunciates, but my home, if you can call it that, is in the Himalayas."

It's true there were so many men like Balanand Baba walking around in Rishikesh, barefoot or in sandals, that I wouldn't indulge in engaging in a conversation with most of them, but something told me to stay and hear what this guy had to say.

"So, where did you learn Vedic astrology?" I asked.

"Ha! 'Vedic' astrology—I believe only a Westerner could have given it that term. In India, so much stems from that Vedic era and these things are the basis of our everyday lives here," he said. I smiled in agreement. "My father was an engineer too, and he was an insightful astrologer. I grew up around him giving readings to friends and family, and so I absorbed it from a very young age."

"It's true that in India, science and spirituality co-exist so casually," I remarked. "You just never know what gifts people carry. It never ceases to amaze me the number of times I've come across a person sitting next to me, someone who looks so normal, and yet they turn out to be highly gifted in an area you would least expect."

The Digital Monk smiled. "Now, can I ask you a question? It might sound strange, and you can decline to tell me if you don't wish to."

Now I was curious. What could he possibly want to know from me? "No worries," I replied. "Fire away."

He shuffled in his seat. "When I was standing behind you in the bookshop, I had a sudden flash of images, like snapshots, of something from the past and I'm sure something in your energy triggered me seeing those things. I mean, I think those snapshots are somehow related to you." He looked at me, not quite sure whether to take the conversation further. I smiled at him, conveying that I was willing to hear what he had to say.

"Have you ever seen any of your past lives?" He looked a little awkward. "It's just that, something tells me that you have." He hesitated, then said, "It's just that, I can see a man on the high seas, in a decorated naval officer's uniform. And something tells me that this person was somehow associated with you." He looked at me, a little nervous, and finished his sentence, "In a previous life."

How amazing was this? How could he know?

"Gosh! Whatever made you come up with that?" I replied, my jaw dropping in surprise. I thought he was going to ask me the typical, banal questions that people in India always asked me, like if I was married. This was the last thing I expected. "How could you know that? Yes, I have been shown a past life of such a person as you're describing," I said, gobsmacked, but not wanting to tell him more just yet.

"Well, I don't know. I just have this image that I'm seeing in my mind's eye, and something tells me very strongly that this has to do with you. This man, this navy commander, came into that lifetime with a thirst for discovering the secrets of the soul. His intuitive and mystical capacities were already well developed from yet another previous life. He had lucid moments of being deeply connected to the Self," Balanand Baba said, his words flowing like the River Ganga beside us.

I remained silent, hooked, unable to wait to hear what he might say next.

"This man travelled far and wide, looking to the stars in the cosmos for his answers," he continued. "It's as if he needed proof of what he felt within and, not finding his answers in the skies, he then turned to mathematics. He was a keen mathematician and worked with some of the leading mathematical brains of his time. With the blessings that were his *karma* of that lifetime, he travelled from one end of the globe to the other, rose to high ranks in his work and his academic endeavours, thoroughly using up the grace of those Jupiterian and Mercurial *karma*. If you were to look in your birth chart now, I should think your Jupiter and Mercury are not your strongest planets," he stopped for breath. My eyes almost popped out of my face. "I am pretty sure that I'm talking about you, in the very life before this one. Do you know what time you were born? I'll make up your birth chart on my computer, if that's all right with you, and tell you if what I'm seeing had any substance."

I was astounded. How could this man, whose name I barely knew, how could he know all this about me? I had not shared these sorts of details with even my closest friends, thinking it would sound too far-fetched and weird, even to those who knew me well. I gave him the information he needed to make my chart.

"There, you see, your Jupiter and Mercury, both retrograde, are in the houses and signs that are not ideal for their placement. From what I just saw of your previous life, you must have had a strong Jupiter, and that had you travel extensively, and your travels would have somehow helped you to gain higher knowledge, including spiritual knowledge. It would have also helped you to rise to the highest ranks in your career. And this time, as much as you may be drawn to the things you did then, you will find that there simply isn't the scope or opportunity for it. Is that correct?" he said, taking a bite of his yak cheese sandwich, which had just been brought to our table.

"This man, he seemed to be well known. Did you get his name when you saw this past life?" he asked.

"Yes, I did. I know his name. It's Xavier de Jourdain. And I know when and where he was born."

"Well, what are you waiting for? Give that to me as well and we'll see if there are any clues or commonality in your charts."

My heart skipped a beat at the thought of what this might show.

Whereas for a long time, I had completely dismissed Vedic astrology as being invalid, more recently I had come to realise that it was an incredibly deep art, possibly even a science, and the reason why most people who claimed to know something about it came up short was because they had not taken the time and effort to delve into learning from its vastness. More recently, it had gripped me, like reading a huge thriller that needed you to pay attention to every detail, the plot, its characters, the small clues, and to look at even the obvious details from multiple perspectives. Much like anything properly researched, only then might you be able to glean something from it of real value.

As he looked at my chart, much like a detective, piecing together a multitude of clues to solve a puzzle, he remarked, "This is fascinating. Your Mars and Moon are both in exactly the same sign and *nakshatra* or star constellation. Both the Moons in your birth chart and his are almost to the same degree, and Mars is less than seven degrees apart in the two charts. Given how many permutations of planetary combinations and star constellations there can be, this is noteworthy."

I looked on, fascinated. Had I not had some understanding through my own study of what made these 'coincidences' noteworthy, it would have just passed me by, like a wave of the Ganges over my head.

"The situations you attract, the work you do, and the challenges that you face, are all shaped so that you have opportunities to strengthen the qualities represented by these particular planets," he said.

"How do you mean? I mean, in the previous lifetime, de Jourdain became a senior naval officer, so he very much used and developed the qualities of action and courage that are depicted by Mars. His Pisces Moon was much where mine is now, so no doubt this would have given him an intuitive and mystical mind. These qualities must have been active within him, too?" I asked.

"Yes, but perhaps in a different way. We'll come to that in a while. You have told me, and so we have the benefit of knowing, that he was an intellectual who worked his way up to the highest ranks within the Navy, that he developed a keen interest in astronomy while he travelled the globe and on those long sea voyages, and he not only studied the stars, but also became an academic in mathematics. Correct? Would you agree that we know all this?" Balanand Baba asked.

"Yes, this we know," I replied.

"Okay. But it's what you haven't told me that's of most interest to me, because it's in looking there that we will find out why knowing about this past life is of any use to you. You see, when you are shown past lives, it's not just casual or for the sake of it. There's always a higher purpose to it. And what is that? It's to show you either what you must heal from that lifetime to move forward in this life, or it's to show you the direction in which you must continue to develop yourself in this lifetime," Balanand Baba said. I listened, fascinated. "So, let's keep looking to see what else we can find here."

The Digital Monk was engrossed in studying Xavier de Jourdain's chart when one of the hundreds of monkeys that freely roamed the streets of Rishikesh, and who made the cables of the swinging bridges and electricity wires their jungle playground, swung past us and suddenly swiped away the monk's half-eaten yak cheese sandwich.

"What the ... ," the surprised monk exclaimed. I laughed at the unspoken expletives that might have fallen out of the monk's mouth, which had him burst out laughing, too. "Oh well ... let that be another one for Lord Hanuman."

I joked. "Hahaha! You're not the monk who sold his Ferrari but the monk who gave away his sandwich, a *yak cheese* sandwich, no less!"

We had a good laugh and he got back to staring at de Jourdain's chart and said, "Looking at his chart, you can see that this man had Moon, Jupiter, Saturn and *Rahu* or the North Node in Pisces. This immediately tells me that we are at the very least looking at a person who is a deep seeker for the truth of his soul. He's someone who has mystical inclinations and he may have experienced his inner being at quite a profound level. Jupiter and Moon in the same sign and house together would have given him a mind (Moon) primed to receiving the higher knowledge with the grace of its great friend, Jupiter. As you know, Jupiter represents higher learning and knowledge, but also long-distance travel. Looking at his chart, with Jupiter, representing large vehicles such as ships, and with Moon in the watery Pisces, it makes sense that he would have been more attracted to water rather than the land-based army."

He stopped for a moment and looked at some calculations that the software on his computer had made. Meanwhile, I asked, "Would it be fair to say that because his *Rahu*, or the North Node, is in conjunction within four degrees of his Jupiter, he could never get enough of it, like he would have yearned for long-distance travel, especially with Jupiter in its own sign of Pisces? And the North Node creating a craving for foreign shores, cultures, and people too?" I asked, trying to understand de Jourdain's, and my own past, better.

"Very much so. And notice that Jupiter is aspecting Scorpio nine houses away, another watery sign and one that would awaken in him the desire to go into the depths of the mystery of life. Why is all this significant? Here's why: this man was not just a scholar and a leader, he was fundamentally a seeker. He was seeking the truth about what he felt and knew through his very well developed intuitive and mystical capacities. *He wanted to prove them through the intellect.* And he seemed to turn to astronomy and mathematics to do so," Balanand Baba said. "In the good old tradition of Copernicus, Galileo and Newton."

"So, would it be fair to say that instead of trusting or having faith in his innate experience of the inner Self, he might have battled with it? Perhaps that was why he felt the need to look far and wide, literally, in the world and outside, in the cosmos, and then through the one area of academia that, in the end, is where scientists have to turn—the area of higher mathematics, to prove the existence of something?"

"That could well be," Balanand Baba said. "Now, look here, your Jupiter and Mercury, they're not bad but they are indeed challenging you in this lifetime. Can you see why?" he asked. I gave him my explanation, from what I understood of the placements of planets and their aspects in my chart.

"Exactly," he agreed. "It tells me something important about the qualities that you are here to develop in this lifetime, as opposed to what you learnt and did in that previous life. You may want to use your intellect to make sense of your intuitive and inner experiences but this time, and your chart shows it, your lesson is to stop looking outside of yourself for validation. Last time round, you went deep into intellectual research, hoping to prove what may never be proven.

"I can tell you, also, that you did not in that lifetime die with the satisfaction of finding the secrets of your soul. Though you had the mystical inklings, you looked outside of yourself for your Self and, therefore, you did not discover it. This time, you are seeking for the answers within, isn't that so?" He searched my face for clues.

"Yes, you can say that." Then I decided to open up more candidly. "Very much so."

"There is yet another lifetime whose imprints you are working through this time also," Balanand Baba said, looking at my chart. "And this one involves your mother— see here, shown by this planet here in your fourth house." He pointed to my chart on his computer screen.

No kidding! How could he see all this?

He must have read the questions on my face because he replied, "As part of my *sadhana*, my *yogic* practice, I have been graced with a knowledge of the *Vedas*, including astrology, and my inner sight has become stronger since I have taken *sanyas* (monkhood). But do not be alarmed. I am often guided to helping souls to connect the dots of their past and present lives, to help them resolve their *karma*. Having said that, this can only happen when the fruits of their *karma* ripen, ready for consumption." As Balanand Baba spoke, I sensed the purity and selflessness of his intention. He had somehow found himself in Rishikesh at the same time as me, this being only my second trip to this special place in my adult years, and somehow we had been in the Ganga Bookstore at exactly the same time.

"What would have happened if I'd declined to speak with you? What if I had indulged my cynical mind and dismissed you as a mad *sadhu*?" I asked.

"Then, you would have missed the opportunity to tie up some *karmic* loose ends that needed to be tied up now, and you would have had to wait for another moment in the future for life to give you yet another avenue to resolve it," he said. "It's just a matter of time, you see. And time is all there is. *Time is the biggest illusion of them all.*"

"You mean, time is *Maha Maya*?"

"Hahaha! Yes, very good! Hahaha! *Maha Maya*, very good," he said, tickled pink.

"Tell me, how can the positioning of the stars and the planets determine or influence what happens to a person in their life?" I asked the question that had always puzzled me. "I mean, if you are carrying all these imprints from your past lives and you're also a reflection of *Atman*, the higher Self, then how does it all work? And how does it all fit together?"

"Ah, you see, the stars do not actually determine what happens to a person. Your birth chart is the blueprint of the sum total of your *karma* and potential. It's a depiction of the person, of your inclinations, based on these two things, your *karma* and potential, at this point in your evolution. The stars and the planets in the sky are just doing what they do, hanging there in the cosmos; they are not exerting any special power over you."

"Then why do people look to the stars for predictions of their future?" I asked.

"You see, your birth chart is like a vault that has a numeric combination lock. When the pattern of the stars and planets are in the right place for the next journey of your soul, everything clicks into place and your soul starts a new life in a new body. Then, throughout your life, as each number clicks into place, the door to the vault opens further, and lets you in to enjoy the fruits of your *karma* or to learn more from it. Of course, some fruits may not be to your liking. But these have nothing to do with the planets or the *nakshatra* or star constellations they are placed in. These star constellations are merely patterns and positioning of the planets and stars that the *rishis* perceived from earth. They then went on to describe them, through their patterns and planet positions and so on. The point is, just as these stars and planets evolve, so do you, as does the entire vast universe," Balanand Baba paused to see if I was following. I nodded.

While pointing to the River Ganges, he said, "Just as if you were to step into the Mother Ganga right at this moment, you would be stepping in and being carried into the trajectory of her flow in this very moment. So it is when you are born. So it is when you are born at a particular moment. You flow into the slipstream of the planetary and stellar patterns that are prevalent at that moment in the cosmos, and Mother Ganga carries you and all the stars and planets in her flow."

I had never before seen it this way. "That's a beautiful explanation. So, what you're saying is, just as stars and planets form certain patterns as viewed from the earth, so we, being a microcosm of the universe, create our own patterns that maps into the cosmic framework."

"Right. And we are part of the flow of life, in concert with the greater cosmos, like a cosmic Mother Ganga with all the galaxies, stars, planets, and living beings flowing together. During the course of that flow, you will encounter rocks and currents and other friction at times, but you cannot go for too long against the flow. So from that view, that of understanding how these patterns function, you can make certain predictions with respect to how that flow will impact an individual's life," he said. I was silent, really impressed with looking at astrology in this way. It made sense that we were all part of the one cosmos, evolving, and that we were part of a greater flow, inside of which it was indeed possible to predict how certain junctures would impact us.

"The soul inhabits human forms so that it can undertake *karma* or actions that will lead to its liberation from the imprints of desires and trauma that have accumulated on the mind, the senses, and the body."

"These act as layers of mud that obscure the brilliant diamond of the soul?" I asked.

"Correct. And so, as the soul comes into body, the mind needs to learn the qualities that will eventually enable it to set itself, and therefore the soul, free from the bondage of *karma's* constant action and reaction, cause and effect. Now, what do the planets and stars have to do with that?" the monk asked.

"Well, we are stardust. The planets, the stars and us, we're comprised of the same elements," I said.

"Exactly. India's ancient seers saw the way the planets and stars functioned in the cosmos," Balanand Baba said. "Each planet has certain qualities and was attributed specific aspects of human life. So, in each lifetime, the mind learns to embody the various qualities represented by a given planet. So, let's say, in the case of Xavier de Jourdain, he learnt to use the qualities and attributes represented by Jupiter and Mercury and, through his Mars, he was in action with warrior-like courage and adventurous spirit, venturing to places new and marshalling lands acquired as part of the French empire. So, in this lifetime, there is little use for you to tread over the same territory. To make progress towards liberation, you will continue by developing other qualities."

"So, if we compare my birth chart with de Jourdain's, we both have the same Mars and Moon, in the same signs, in the same *nakshatra* star constellations and almost to the same degrees. Would it be fair to say that instead of going to find proof outside for the inner Self that I experience so strongly—I call it my Inner Diamond—I need to find the courage to trust it, to develop *shraddha*, faith, in my experience?"

"Very good. That could certainly be one aspect of your learning this time. Mars rules over your chart and casts a favourable aspect to the Moon, its friend. So, you could say that this time, you would do well to have the courage not so much to fight on warships or on the battlefield of the ocean, but to be the spiritual warrior or pioneer or adventurer, charting and conquering inner territories of the mind and mystical heart, the bridge to the higher Self. Then, share what you learn with whomsoever is ready to do so for themselves, and counsel or teach them to get in touch with their inner being. This I can see from your chart," he said, as I took in his words.

"Where does it all end?" I asked. "I mean, if time is infinite and the soul is eternal, then where does it all end?"

The monk laughed out loud. "You've just told the cosmic joke of all time! Haha!" he said, plucking his beard.

He looked at me and realised that this was not a rhetorical question. I was waiting for his answer. "Well, you see, we are dealing with the vault of the heavens, remember? The same one as I mentioned before. The dial combination will click into place to bring you into your next life; it will keep you coming into new bodies for as long as you have more learning to do that will enable you to work through each one of your *karma*. Remember, the planets and stars of the Indian astrology are nothing more than patterns at the time of your birth, and through life, that enable you to engage in actions that will ultimately release you from being trapped in a *karmic* cycle of birth and rebirth. So, when you have consciously integrated the qualities of these outer planets and stars with your own inner essence, and this will coincide with the moment when you have burnt your *karma*, both pleasant and challenging, the cycle will be complete."

"So, in that moment, the dial will finally arrive at the correct combination to unlock the vault of the heavens, so to speak, releasing me from the wheel of *karma*?" I asked, seeing a huge celestial vault finally opening, after lifetimes of trial and error.

"That's a great image. It's something like that. Certainly, all the planets and star constellations will be where they need to be, personally to you, to enable your liberation." The monk smiled. "And that is the case for each and every one of us, without exception. Some take longer than others to complete their cycle."

"What happens after your soul is liberated? You don't hang out in some mythical heaven eating figs and grapes all day long though, do you?" I giggled.

"Then, my dear, you have *real* choice. What you choose to do with your time is between you and eternity," he replied with a dry sense of humour, but I understood what he meant.

"There's something so right and magical about this theory, at least for me," I said. "I now better understand how our personal astrology aligns with the planets and star constellations. They're depicted symbolically in Vedic philosophy and, in each lifetime, we learn more and more to embody and integrate the qualities of each of the nine planets."

The Baba nodded in approval. "These cosmic entities and patterns reflect both the darkness and light of the cosmos and, therefore, our own soul's essence. The so-called *tamasic* or malefic planets—Saturn, Mars and the nodes—are not negative at all. Indeed, they hold the very essence or seeds of our light."

Balanand Baba added, "Without darkness, light cannot emerge and light alone would merely cause combustion."

"Therefore," I said, jumping further into the flow of the conversation, "our lesson is to learn to consciously integrate, through awareness and acceptance, these two opposites—darkness and light. In doing so, you are able to actualise their power by bringing them into a *sattvic* or pure balance within you."

I took in a deep breath, enjoying this exceptional conversation from a very unusual, seemingly random meeting. I paused for a minute, letting it all soak in. "Well, what do you know! I wondered all along why I had been shown that lifetime of Vice Admiral de Jourdain. I mean, it wasn't traumatic or anything. When I saw it, I didn't understand what from that lifetime remained unresolved and how I could put to good use what I had seen from it. Now, with what you've just brought to light, I get it. I need to trust in my mystical experiences and to be at peace with it all. I simply need to accept the higher Self's existence and become one with it in my every thought, my every action. This time, it's all about trusting myself, about *shraddha*, faith. Wow! This is extraordinary," I said. Balanand Baba just smiled.

I continued, "*This* was what I've come here searching for—why I had to make this trip to India! It's to gain a conscious knowing of how I could build on what I had learnt in my lifetime previous to this one. I realise that the severe bouts of doubting myself, my mystical tendencies and experiences, are remnants from my previous life as Xavier de Jourdain, and I now need to go beyond that doubt, to develop a rock solid trust and faith in those capacities that grant me these experiences."

"This time round, yes, with both your Jupiter and Mercury retrograde—and that's exactly what they will demand of you, and they certainly fortify these challenges for you to overcome," Balanand Baba said.

I was exhilarated with making this connection to my previous incarnation, and seeing why I had to make this trip to Rishikesh and, more relevantly, what in this lifetime my Inner Diamond was asking me to learn.

"Thank you so much for this enlightening conversation, Babaji," I said with heartfelt gratitude. "How can I repay you for everything that you've just told me?"

"Well, for one, you can buy me a coffee and another yak cheese caprese sandwich," Balanand Baba grinned. "I do love those little sandwiches."

"The ancient Indian seers
saw at
the core of the human being
a brilliant, inextinguishable light,
like a sparkling diamond.
They called this diamond 'Atman',
higher consciousness ...
and it lives within us
in its
essence."

23

Pujya Swamiji

The time had come to head on to the Parmarth Niketan Ashram, where I hoped the monk-saint that I had seen in my dream would be present. It had proven difficult beforehand to find out for sure if he would be in town or travelling, though I had tried telephoning the *ashram* before leaving London. I made my way across the river by walking along the swinging bridge, Lakshman Jhula, and arrived on the opposite side to the Ganga Bookstore and German Bakery. The bridge was heaving with people scurrying across, cows blocking parts of the narrow passage on the bridge—oblivious to the frantic crowd—and monkeys dangling from the suspension cables, poised to swipe whatever food they could from passers-by.

After the short walk to the *ashram*, through the narrow alley full of little souvenir shops along the river, I found my way inside the *ashram* complex and to the reception. I explained to the man at the counter that I had come from London, England, and enquired if Swami Chidanand Saraswatiji was in town, and whether it was at all possible to meet with him. Not really sure what to expect, I thought he was going to turn me away, but instead, he very politely asked me to take a seat while he left his desk for a minute or two. He returned quickly. "Please, follow me. I will introduce you to Sadhviji."

He took me to an office where, to my surprise, a beautiful woman with a mane of long curly brown hair, clad in a cotton orange nun's *sari* got up from behind her large wooden desk and stepped out to greet me. Though I didn't know who she was then, I immediately recollected having seen a photo of her in the same magazine in which I had seen Pujya Swamiji's picture.

"*Jai Shri Krishna*. Welcome to Parmarth," she said in an American accent, beaming brightly.

"*Jai Shri Krishna*," I replied. "Thank you for seeing me, Sadhviji. I hope I'm not disturbing you. I wasn't sure if it was at all a possibility to meet with Swamiji, and your colleague kindly brought me in to meet with you."

She smiled. "Is this your first time to Parmarth? How did you hear about us?"

I was captivated by the openness in her demeanour and, more than that, she emanated a radiance that I just could not miss. Going by the various piles of papers in her office, it was clear she was busy with several projects at once that demanded her full attention, and yet she was willing to give me a slice of her time.

"It's a curious thing, Sadhviji," I said. "A few months ago, I had a dream in which I saw this distinguished-looking smiling monk in orange robes. He just smiled at me and placed his hand on my head, blessing me. He left such an impression on me that when I woke up the next morning, he was the first thing that came to my mind. I had no idea who that man was so I didn't think twice about it. The next day, I went to my mother's house to give her the groceries that I had bought for her and, right there, on her sitting room table was the Gujarati magazine, called *Garvi Gujarat*, that she buys on subscription and that had just arrived in her letterbox."

"Ah, yes, *Garvi Gujarat*. We know them well." Sadhviji smiled.

"Do you? Well, on its cover was the face of the same smiling monk in orange clothes that I had seen in my dream. On seeing that same face on the cover of this magazine, I had goosebumps and I opened it to read about who this enigmatic man was. And here I am!"

"Ah well. Let's see if we can have you meet with Pujya Swamiji this evening. Can you stay for the

Ganga Aarti ceremony tonight?" she asked, exuding an unmistakable vibrance.

"Yes, of course. What time is it?" I asked.

"It will be at around seven o'clock. Look, in the meantime, before the *aarti*, there's a *havan*, a sacred fire ceremony, taking place at the riverside. Why don't you participate? I'll ask someone to take you there right now," she said. A genuine lightness and enthusiasm pervaded Sadhviji's being, and I couldn't help being touched and moved. She picked up the phone and, to my utter surprise, in perfect Hindi laced with ever such a slight American accent, she said, *"Jaraa meri office me aaieyegaa,"* (can you please come into my office?). Then, again speaking into the phone, still in perfect Hindi, she said, "And bring two cups of hot spiced tea also."

"Oh my goodness!" My eyes and mouth both wide open, I gawped like a fish underwater. "You speak Hindi! And you speak so fluently. That's amazing. I don't know hardly any Westerners who have learnt to do that. Wow. I'm *so* impressed." And I genuinely was.

I could read, write and speak Hindi and Gujarati fluently, and so by default, could read and write Sanskrit too. I had studied German at school and English and French to college level, and so I knew how different these languages were to the Indian languages. Besides, becoming fluent in a language was not just about the vocabulary and grammar, or stringing sentences together. To become fluent, you had to get a grasp on the culture too, and I could tell that she had painstakingly been able to do that. It was obvious that Sadhviji was exceptionally bright.

Sadhvi Bhagwati Saraswati, the name given to her by Swamiji, was born to Jewish American parents and had led a blessed life in Los Angeles, California. I learnt that she had a doctorate from the Ivy League university of Stanford, and had qualified as a neurologist. During a trip to India, she visited Rishikesh and, standing on the banks of the River Ganga, she experienced for the first time the profound sense of 'being home', and this one experience altered the course of her life. She went back to California to complete her PhD and soon after returned to give her life to the study of the Self and to making her life about being of service. I liked this woman. She was smart and genuine, a powerhouse.

After a few sips of chai, I was led through the *ashram* grounds and down the steps of the River Ganga by an enthusiastic young man to whom Sadhviji had given instructions to take me to the fire ceremony. People from all over the world were seated on the steps that led down to the river, watching the proceedings. On the platform just in front of the riverbank, were a couple of young priests in yellow clothes, with a family of Indians. They sat around the square firepit that was being kept ablaze with regular offerings of *ghee* butter and sticks of wood. The young man who had taken me to them told the priest that I was to participate in the fire ceremony and, before I knew it, I was in full flow of making offerings to the fire and chanting the *mantras* for, what I learnt, was a *Maha Mritunjaya* ceremony. *Mrityu*, meant death, *jaya*, meant victory, and *Maha Mritunjaya*, a form of Lord Shiva—the transformer, who is said to have the power to grant life to a dying man. This sacred fire ceremony was being conducted to seek the blessing of good health and life.

India never ceased to amaze me with its abundant generosity. Here was I, sitting here, quite unexpectedly through Sadhviji's wonderful grace, on the banks of the sacred-most river of my culture. How could life be any better? A sense of feeling complete and fulfilled soaked me, as I stepped into the spiritual flow of the Ganga beside me, sharing this wonderful ceremony with strangers who, as it turned out, were a family from Rajasthan and happened to live in Ahmedabad, in the same neighbourhood as my cousin Avinash.

We continued to make offerings for more than an hour as we waited with anticipation for Pujya Swamiji to arrive and start the *Ganga Aarti*. The sun had nearly descended over the horizon. At the entrance, where the wide steps made a descent to the riverbank, two particularly mischievous monkeys on the rooftops of the small buildings beside the steps caught my eye. Just above the entrance was an arch, on top of which was a magnificently carved, enormous horse-drawn chariot carrying Lord Krishna and the great warrior Arjun. It depicted the scene from the battlefield on which these two had a conversation that became the *Bhagavad Gita*. A tall flagpole sat atop the chariot, and a white flag floated out from it.

The more mischievous of the two monkeys jumped from the right roof onto the flagpole and shook it to its heart's content, screaming loudly, completely oblivious to the sacredness of the scene which he was disrupting. I could not help laughing out loud at seeing that even Lord Krishna himself was being shaken up by a naughty monkey, jumping from the flagpole and then to sit inside the chariot, in the lap of Krishna himself, and then onto the horse and then to the lion that was following the chariot. The two monkeys fought from time to time for the prize of being at the very top of the flagpole. The monkeys, it seemed, were having the time of their lives.

The young, yellow-clad *rishikumars* (students) of Pujya Swamiji, prepared the *ghee*-lit lamps and ushered the hordes of people that were arriving to participate in the *Ganga Aarti* ceremony. It seemed that Pujya Swamiji was held up elsewhere, and while we waited for him, one of the female renunciates and a monk with a harmonium and another with a pair of *tabla* drums kicked off the chanting of devotional songs, *bhajans*. Three to four hundred people, Indians and citizens of the globe, joined in, chanting the lines of the well-known songs as best as they could. The *ghee* lamps flickered in the still humidity of the falling night, lighting up the riverbank with hope and possibility.

I sensed a special kind of harmony from the poetic words and sentiments of the devotional songs being chanted. Even in the subtle spaces between the lines of a song, there was a special kind of peace. Like dots that joined up and made sense of a seemingly impossible conundrum, each and every person present in the sharing of this special experience was effortlessly connected to each other.

Then, instead of the familiar voices that had been leading the chants, another voice took charge. It was a beautiful, rich voice, filled with deep *bhava*, an authentic feeling that, the moment I heard this voice, pressed a button that had my heart fling wide open. I turned around and there he was, Pujya Swamiji, the monk whom I had seen in my dream and that had me come to the banks of the Ganga. For a being of such giant spiritual stature, I was surprised to find that he was much shorter than I had imagined. But what a towering impression he made! After singing the *Ganga Aarti*, Pujya Swamiji addressed the gathering, speaking about a current affairs issue that was grabbing the headlines of the day. Enriched all the more by the sophistication of the Hindi language, I was struck by the beauty of Pujya Swamiji's speech. The way he weaved his words and sentences together were almost poetic. This man, being, saint—call him what you will—had the presence of someone authentic through and through. The real McCoy. Involuntary tears of joy welled up in my eyes as I experienced his presence and clarity of energy. I had never been one to look up to celebrities, or been allowed by my Inner Diamond to follow any external *gurus*, and yet, here I was: touched and moved by the presence of Pujya Swamiji.

An hour later, as the *Ganga Aarti* came to a close, one of the yellow-clad *rishkumars* found me in the crowd and asked me to follow him into the *ashram*, where Pujya Swamiji would be appearing for giving *darshan*, a personal audience, to a few people. It was a humble room with an adobe-type floor, on which a handful of people were already seated. The *rishikumar* sat me in the front, to the left of where Puyja Swamiji's mat had been laid. This whole evening felt like a dream to me, similar to the one in which I had first glimpsed this swami. How did I end up here? I couldn't wipe off my smile.

Pujya Swamiji walked in with Sadhviji, and the room fell silent and still, to hear the subtlest thought and soak up every word that this modern-day sage had to offer. I looked at Sadhviji, who emitted her own radiance. Once the two of them settled into their floor seats, Pujya Swamiji connected with each person in the room by looking at their faces, and smiling softly. He warmly acknowledged a few individuals whom he evidently recognised.

"Who has the first question?" Pujya Swamiji asked, looking around the room. No one moved. A middle-aged Indian man then raised his hand, and Pujya Swamiji nodded at him to go ahead with his question.

"Swamiji, I'm working really hard and I realise that I'm very stressed, yet still, I'm afraid of not being successful enough."

Pujya Swamiji smiled. "There is a beautiful Sanskrit *mantra* that we used a lot when I was a young monk, living in the jungle: *jitam jagat kena mano hi yena*. In such a small sentence, Sanskrit manages to create a whole world. This one *mantra* gives you the answer to all the hindrances that we face in our human drama—fear of failure, the pain and anguish of loss, jealousy, guilt, selfishness, and all the other conditions we come across every day." He looked at the man who had asked the question, and then around the room.

"*Jagat* means the world, the universe. *Jit* is to conquer," Pujya Swamiji said to a rapt audience. "To conquer what or whom, though? Someone else outside? Are you fighting with someone else? Is your fight with another? *Tam is* darkness. The darkness of what? This darkness is the darkness of ignorance. We don't have to wage war against this darkness, because it exists only for one reason: our own ignorance. Your own ignorance. All you have to do is to light the candle and *jitam*, victory, will be yours immediately. And what is this lighting of the candle? It's the switching on of your awareness, the awareness of the Self that comes through your own higher mind."

Pujya Swamiji paused for a few moments, looking around the room, resting his serene gaze on different faces, pierced by a shining, almost fierce, brightness of his eyes. A layman could easily mistake someone with such softness of demeanour to be a walkover, but he would be entirely misguided. Such monks were nothing less than true scholars and hardcore *yogis*. To achieve such softness and tenderness of heart required letting go of more than most are able to imagine, and lifelong *tapasya*, a deep, long, discipline of spiritual practice and development of inner focus, often in extended periods of hermit-solitude.

"When I was a young monk, I lived in the jungle. There was no course in the jungle for stress management. There was no food to eat, no restaurant, no shopping centres, no hospital—we had nothing there. You could keep being stressed about anything. Nothing was secure. In fact, there were many reasons to be insecure. Zero security, fear all the time—animals, lions, snakes ... you couldn't even sleep. I remember that we had to wrap our shawls around us in such a way ..." Swamiji took his shawl and wrapped it tightly beneath both his feet, so that he looked like a wrapped burrito, and then lifted it to look inside his wrapped shawl. "And in mid-sleep, feeling a creepy-crawly moving beneath us, we would wake up, and look to find that it was a deadly scorpion. We would pick it up, move it away, and go back to sleep." Swamiji let out a laugh, his smile revealing white, even teeth. The room laughed with him.

Addressing the man whose question he was answering, Pujya Swamiji added, "That was in the jungle, but the same is happening in your life, every minute of every day. Fear is all over. No security. No Chi-Chi's, no McDonald's. Where to go for food? You didn't know where to go for food, even. We were not allowed to pick fruit from trees. So if fruit fell from the trees, we ate. If not, we went without. No problem. There are stories of monks who found no fallen fruit for days on end, and they went without food because they had taken a vow that only if fruit falls from trees of its own accord would they eat it. They said, 'If the Divine wants to satisfy my hunger, He will send the fruit'. Otherwise, they made no effort even to quench their thirst or remove their hunger." I took in Swamiji's amazing parable, feeling quite embarrassed about my own pathetic, demanding nature.

"There were so many reasons to be stressed," Swamiji continued, "but still, there was no stress management course in the jungle. Not once did I find even just one monk being stressed or being worried. Never did I once find in the jungle even a board with the words 'stress management course'." The audience laughed. "Nowhere. Not even for free, let alone paying dollars for such a course. The only thing we had was *awareness*. We would recite this *mantra, jitam jagat kena mano hi yena: Self management*." He stopped to take a sip of water from a steel cup.

"Through newspapers and magazines, and television and BlackBerries, and Internet and gossip, we are watching what others are doing. But those monks and *rishis* in the jungle, they were not worried about others, saying, 'What are those other monks and animals up to?' They were not concerned with managing their stress or their worries. They had concerns, but only about one thing: how to bring happiness to others. Not even one *mantra* have I found, in my entire life, going through countless scriptures, that says, 'Oh Lord, make me happy'. Not one. Those *rishis* were praying for one thing and one thing only: May *all* be happy. They were not worried about what other people were doing, but they were concerned about how those others could be happy, how they could be at peace, how they could be free from suffering and pain; that was their preoccupation, not how can they learn to reduce their stress levels."

Pujya Swamiji continued, "So, if not stress management, then how to deal with stress and fear? How to take your attention away from those things that consume your attention on a minute-by-minute basis? Our ancient *rishis* worked to discover how to become one with Self, how to become one with the universe, because they knew it was then that all your stress, all your suffering, all your selfishness, would disappear in a puff of smoke. But how to bring this Self awareness? For that, the *rishis* created not stress management but Self Management."

I looked around the room, at the faces of people who clearly were in awe of this famed Indian saint, and wondered how these gems of wisdom were impacting their worlds. Swamiji's counsel seemed simple enough: go within and develop the muscle, the discipline to shine the light of your higher Self's awareness onto your dark thoughts and fears. Let its light fill you with the knowing that there is nothing to fear but fear itself, and give yourself to serving something other than your petty needs and fears. Let go of being consumed by 'my needs', 'my fears', 'my success', 'my life'. Serve the Self by choosing some higher purpose and let the Self guide your every move, your every step—and see how those small, small worries disappear. Simple, yet I wondered why was it so hard to let go of being consumed by our egos?

Everyone in the room, attentively taking in Pujya Swamiji's teaching, knew that what he was saying was right, and I for one felt the futility of a life that was only for myself. I wanted to do more, I wanted to *be* more, but how? As if hearing my thoughts, Swamiji said, "But how to become more Self aware? How to do this in our everyday lives? Where do you start? Well, for one thing, stop looking outside of yourself at what others are doing, and comparing, and bring your attention within, towards your Self. Take care of your Self, not of what others are doing or are not doing. Let that not be any of your business.

"So, how to bring this Self awareness into your daily lives? You might say that if I am not there, if my ego is not there, then how will I ever become successful? So you participate in a drama, the drama that is your life, *my* life, you say. Believe me, the drama is always on. We are in a drama anyway. We each are playing a role in some drama or other but, in that drama, we are one mere actor. Know that there is a Director, while we are merely playing the role of what you call *I* or *me*. The problem comes when we begin to believe that we are the drama. We are not. The *rishis* gave the *sutras* that said, 'You are not the drama, you are merely acting in one'. That Director has given you a role to play in this drama. Lucky you are, that he has given you a role, that you are something. It's when we take that role and start rolling others," he said, making high circles in the air with his index finger, "then it becomes a problem. We just have to play our own role. Because of my drama, my desires, my expectations, I make myself insecure and miserable and then, when I am insecure and miserable about myself, I make others' lives miserable. I blame my misery on others and then they must be made to suffer. Play your own role. Only your own. So you go from *koham*, who am I, to *soham*, I am That, I am all that is."

He turned to the middle-aged Indian man who had said that he worked hard, felt stressed, and was afraid that he might be unsuccessful. "So, how can you doubt yourself? *Soham*, when you are connected to the Self, you are All That Is." Pujya Swamiji threw his hands up in the air and concluded, "Where is the question of possibly being unsuccessful?"

He stayed silent for a few seconds, and then looked at a young girl, a teenager, whom he seemed to know. "It's okay, Komal, you can ask me anything you like." The teenager, encouraged by Pujya Swamiji's recognition, said, "I feel worthless. You do so much for people and you've been doing it since you were young. But I do so little. I'm just worthless. How will I ever do anything with my life?"

Pujya Swamiji smiled at her with compassion and replied, "You must start where you are. You don't have to solve world hunger, just do what you can. But do your best and leave the rest to God. That, you will find, is good enough for Him. What you do, devote it all to Him. Let it be your offering to the Divine. Taking small, small steps, doing small—small is good. It keeps you humble. Humility is the first sign that God is within you. God appreciates the little things that you do, because that too, is part of the big plan. It is only from the small, little steps that anything big ever happens. Remember what I said earlier about looking outside of yourself and comparing. Don't do that. It's a trap. You will never find what you are here to do if you look outside. Carry on learning, carry on enquiring, *deham naham koham soham*. *Deham*, the body; *na*, not; *aham*, I; I am not the body (and the ego). *Koham?* Who am I? *Soham*: you are That, the Self. It will surely emerge."

Another teenager, an Indian youth this time, plucked up the courage to ask his question. "I have to succeed in my exams because I don't want to disappoint my parents. They do so much for me. I want to grow up and earn a lot of money and make them proud. But I also want to do all the things you talk about and I want to travel the world, too. I'm so confused about which path to choose. Should I devote my life to working and earning, or should I give it, like you, to learning about the Self and serving people?" How moving, I thought, to see such a young person battling with these mature, existential questions about which many before him have had to make crucial choices, but possibly much later in life.

"Self is everywhere, omnipresent. It merely needs you to turn your attention towards it and it makes itself known to you. Life is not just to learn and earn. Life is to return also. Learning is great but, at the same time, you must make the time, every day, to develop yourself, your relationship with the Self, as full and complete. That is called true blossoming. If you bring this balance into your life, it does not matter whether you are in India or America, a cave or California, because Self is there, where you are. You may learn more and more, your life will go at a fast speed, but there will be no direction. And what is the use of speed without direction? Speed and direction must go together, hand in hand. Getting gold medals is not the aim of life, being a role model is the aim of life. You have to do Self study every day and you become a role model. Go and be brilliant with your studies. Go and look at the Internet all you like. But take care of your inner-net also. Internet and inner-net go hand in hand," Swamiji answered. I was impressed that he was so aware of the World Wide Web. He was indeed a *rishi* of the modern age. The young man appeared relieved at Swamiji's answer and bobbed his head with gratitude.

Pujya Swamiji looked at Sadhviji to see if there was time remaining for any more questions. "One last question then," he said.

"Swamiji, when I'm in this environment, where people meditate and they're so kind, I feel so connected to them, even if I don't know them. I get a wonderful feeling of love and I'm at ease. But when I'm not here, when I'm back at school, with so many different kinds of people, it hurts me because I feel I'm separate from them. Why is that?" asked yet another young girl, who could not have been more than sixteen. Again, it was amazing to see one so young have the awareness and clarity to grapple with such questions with so much concern.

"A very good question. What is your name, little birdie?" Swamiji asked.

"Shreya, Swamiji," she replied in a barely audible voice.

"Shreya, the beautiful, auspicious Goddess Lakshmi. We must learn to meditate everywhere, not just in one corner. Let the whole of life become your meditation, then that feeling of separateness will disappear. *You* will feel connected and one with all around you, and it doesn't matter how others react to you. You will *know*, even if they don't, that you are all one. When your attention is on the Self, then more and more people will come with whom you *can* be connected. Keep asking the right questions, young Shreya, and Self will surely *keep* bringing you the proper answers." Pujya Swamiji placed his right hand on his heart, to bring the question and answer session to a close. One family at a time, people came to pay their respects to him, bowing and touching his feet for his blessings. The scriptures said that to be able to even get a tiny bit of dust off the feet of your parents, elders, or a man of true knowledge, was a matter of good fortune because merely that would elevate your life.

The cardboard cut-out that I used to feel like had disappeared many years ago and the real me had been gradually and cautiously emerging, but I knew that more of who I am would yet surface when the time was right. Basking in the presence of this rare and holy man who had first granted me *darshan*, his vision, in a dream, even my stubborn and inflated ego had melted and gone to heaven.

The room was now empty, except for me, Sadhviji and Pujya Swamiji. He turned to me and asked me my name and where I was from. After I had answered him, something exceptional happened. In the following moments, as Swamiji and I looked at each other, I realised that he 'recognised' me, that he knew who I was and I 'saw' with my inner sight the enormity of who he was. I spontaneously bowed with respect to Pujya Swamiji and felt the warmth of his palm gently on my head, as he granted me his blessing.

In that precious recognition, all my questions faded away and even those ever-mischievous monkeys in my mind, like those prancing around on Krishna and Arjun's chariot in the *ashram* courtyard, surrendered into a peaceful stillness.

Having earlier made a powerful, energetic connection to the sacred Ganges and being in the inspiring presence of this holy man, my heart flung open some more and I experienced a sense of being 'full', like never before. My inner being sprung forth with the quiet joy of wholeness. Not being able to contain this rare state, my eyes welled up, quite involuntarily, and set in motion a flow of tears of *being*, just pure being.

In this state of wholeness, 'it' was enough, I was enough, everything was simply more than *enough*.

24

Life or Death

"It's all f*#@ed up down there! I'm not going to touch you. No one will."

The Scottish surgeon, who had performed an exploratory laparoscopy on me earlier that morning, gave this far from compassionate prognosis. He had popped by to give me his verdict of why I had been experiencing frequent pain in my abdomen.

My good friend Rupin had come by to see me and happened to be sitting at my hospital bedside. I looked at him with the unspoken question, *Did he, this so-called expert in his field, really just say that?* We looked at each other and laughed, thinking the surgeon was a bit of a joker.

"What you've got is a condition that's more complex than a complex cancer, and I'm not going to touch it," the surgeon said, as dispassionate as if he was telling his wife that their supermarket had run out of her favourite brand of peanuts.

"What do you mean?" I asked, utterly confused, more so because I was still under the effect of the general anaesthetic. "Why didn't you operate on me then, while you had me in the operating theatre? Are you saying that I've got a bad cancer?"

"No, no. It's not cancer. That's the good news. The bad news is it could turn into cancer pretty soon, because your condition's already so advanced. More so than anything I've seen. It's a condition that's causing blood to flow in the wrong direction and so it's gluing some of your vital organs together. And there are some other complications," he replied coldly. "There's also lots of tissue growing on top of some of your organs. So all in all, it makes what you've got very difficult, if not impossible, to treat with surgery."

Panic arose. I felt shocked. Worried. Upset. "But why? What's the cause of it?"

"Well, no one knows." His manner was sharp and indifferent.

"What do you mean no one knows? Is it a rare condition? What research has been done on it?" I asked, mustering up the meagre energy I had.

"Well, the condition itself isn't rare but the voracity with which it's occurring in your body is unusual," he replied.

"But what's causing it?"

"It's most likely genetic."

"Is there any treatment for it? I mean, why am in pain more frequently than before?"

"There's no cure for it." He remained curt.

The questions flooded my brain faster than I could synthesise them. I stayed silent, while my stomach churned with panic. Eventually, I asked, "What do you mean you can't operate?" I felt desperate. "When I came to see you for the first time, you told me you were one of the most experienced and the best in the field."

"Well, I am. Twenty years in the field and I've never seen a condition such as yours," he said, callous and matter of fact, as if he was doing me a favour with his expert arrogance.

Rupin and I looked at him, still wondering if this guy was joking.

"It's way out of control and *I'm not going to touch it! No one will.*" The expert surgeon emphasised the last part of his little speech with Gaelic fervour.

I looked at Rupin as we both realised that the surgeon was as serious as a high court judge sentencing a serial criminal.

I was stumped to hear this doctor's prognosis. My world was crumbling and all I could do was stare at him wide-eyed, mouth agape. Every word that came out of the surgeon's mouth felt more excruciating than the pain I had been suffering with, as if I was still on the operating table, pieces of me being chopped out without anaesthetic.

"Look." He glanced at his watch in a gesture of impatience. "I'm going to put you on a course of hormone treatment for the next eighteen months. Let's see if that helps. Though it's highly unlikely, if it does bring about a change in what your insides look like compared to the state they're in now, then we'll review and see if I can operate on you. Come and see me in a couple of days when you're more awake and I'll give you the prescription then." He turned his back on me and marched away.

"Wait, you said this could turn into cancer pretty soon. How long is 'pretty soon'?" I asked, trembling.

He stopped and studied me over his shoulder. "Oh, seeing as how advanced things are in there with so many things stuck together and rampant tissue growth, I'd say within a couple of years at most, or sooner." After casting his confident pronouncement of my death sentence, he continued to stride out of the room. "You're lucky that the tissue growth hasn't spread to your eyes or ears, or away from the pelvis. But that could happen," he called over his shoulder, just before he disappeared from view.

The fear of hell ran savage through me.

Rupin had witnessed the whole scene. He looked at me, his eyes ready to pop out of his head, and clearly echoing my shock. "I know," I said, desolate. "I can't believe that just happened, either."

Along with my body, my spirit felt limp and drained.

It was one thing to be given this kind of life-threatening news in such a callous and ghastly manner, but it was quite another to realise that the balance of my life rested in the hands of this cold-blooded, hammerhead shark-like excuse of a human being. Even comparing him to a hammerhead was doing great disservice to their species because most were harmless to humans. I could not say the same for this surgeon, 'Doctor Hammerhead'.

I left the hospital, hopeless.

This disease had crept up on me with little warning, quiet like the dead of night. I was particular about my diet and keeping fit. Being from Gujarat, I had been brought up a strict vegetarian, eating neither meat nor fish of any kind. While growing up, though, I did go through a phase of experimenting with chicken, cheeseburgers, shrimps, prawns and crabmeat, and could not understand what all the fuss was about. I even found that I felt better without it and so made the choice to remain vegetarian, just as I had been raised.

It would not have been an exaggeration to say that I was a health fanatic. I had only the occasional drink, a glass or two of margarita or half a glass of red wine with a special meal, perhaps four times a year. I had never smoked, never even tried, so a spliff was out of the question, let alone ingesting or injecting anything hardcore. I rarely got headaches or even colds, except once every ten years, so I was especially confounded with this turn of events.

Since the age of seventeen, I had complained about my often unbearable menstrual cramps and pain and unusually heavy blood flow. Why had the local GPs fobbed me off with just painkillers, telling me that my severe bouts of pain were 'normal', that there was nothing to worry about? If things were as bad as they were, why had they assured me that it was perfectly 'normal' to prescribe painkillers consistently, and to take daily, for more than two years? Why had they not thought it necessary to refer me for specialist attention?

How did I develop a condition that was so advanced without my knowledge? Over the coming days, I began to question and doubt myself. Had I been that asleep to what was going on in my body? Had I ignored the signs, battling through the symptoms, getting on with life no matter what? I thought and thought about where I might have missed or ignored a symptom, but could find nothing. For the most part, I had felt healthy, fit and full of vitality, except for three days during my moon cycle. That is, except for the last two years, when I had visited the local GP practice more often than throughout my entire life, complaining of worsening pelvic pain. The GPs hadn't been any more insightful than Doctor Hammerhead, either.

Was this surgeon, claiming to be an expert in the area of my disease, just full of himself, or was he really as experienced as he said he was? How reliable and trustworthy was his prognosis that it was "all f*#@ed up down there"? How could I know? How could I find out how good a doctor he really was? It seemed the local doctors recommended you to the so-called specialist ... and I was supposed to blindly trust my life in his hands? Even if I asked for a second opinion, how could I really know if that doctor was going to be any better than the one I already had? This was a minefield.

There was something seriously wrong with this scenario.

A few days after my exploratory procedure, I went back to Doctor Hammerhead and picked up my prescription.

"So, what happens if your prescribed medicine doesn't work? What then?" I asked, dejected.

"Then you die," he said, quick as a flash. Hungry lions had more empathy for their kill than this so-called physician.

Over the coming months, the cramps and pelvic pain continued and became more unpredictable, unmanageable and urgent. The agony in my pelvis was excruciating, as if set ablaze. The humble hot-water bottle became my constant bed companion, alleviating and soothing the chronic back pain caused by the fiery inflammation-like sensations, which pounded my nervous system.

Other symptoms emerged. On one occasion, I drove with a colleague to a meeting with a large corporate customer for an important business meeting, and had to run out of the meeting three times in one hour to throw up. As soon as I got in my car to go home, the pain started and all I could do was lie down on the back seat, clutching my stomach until the painkillers kicked in and the pain died down, some half an hour later.

It got to the stage that when the pain began, I was in so much agony that I would find myself rolling about on the floor or the bed, groaning or screaming, clutching my knees to my chest and rocking from side to side on my back. I would do whatever it took to bear the pain and wait for it to die down. The pains got so intolerable that the doctors gave me a stronger, morphine-based, painkiller—typically given for consuming over short periods to post-surgery patients. I consulted different doctors to seek a second and third opinion, and none of them seemed to be more insightful than the first. Despite being on three of the stronger medicines for pain management, none of them offered an alternative course of action. Regardless, of one thing I was clear, I was not going to accept being on morphine for the rest of my life and nor did the course of action the doctor had taken sit right with me.

Doctor Hammerhead had put me on heavy doses of medication to see what the effect would be on my condition, to see if it would temper the extreme growth of tissue that was rampaging through my pelvic cavity, covering organs such as my intestines. He wanted to halt my cycle and see if the organs that had been glued together with the excessive blood flowing in the wrong direction might dry up.

After just one month, Doctor Hammerhead's medication made me feel utterly depressed. It felt like poison coursing through my body, draining the life out of me. It made me feel suicidal.

In one of my crisis moments, with sharp, electrical shooting pains striking ceaselessly in all directions within my belly, like thunder and lightening rampaging across the sky, I was no longer sure if this was my disease or the medication that was causing the pain.

It seemed to me that the medication was worse than the disease.

My health had suddenly plummeted into a precarious state and I was at a dead end. Almost no one in my life, including my doctors, understood or could help me with just how bad and serious my condition had become. I had never felt as alone and desolate as now. Already, I'd consulted three experts, including undergoing one exploratory procedure to establish the facts, and didn't know where to go from here.

Though I didn't know of anything better, I refused to accept Doctor Hammerhead's prognosis. There *had* to be another way. I had to find a way of getting to it.

Now, I had only one place to look for the answers: to go within and tap into my higher Self and its infinite creative resourcefulness. There, I was always bound to find the exact solution, and pull forth, effortlessly, the most surprising yet perfect resources.

Though the prognosis seemed bleak, my connection and trust in myself was strong, and I felt adamant that I would rise above this challenge. I felt in the very core of my being that there was sunshine just waiting to burst through on the other side of this tunnel.

"If I am going to die, then I refuse to suffer excruciating pain until my last breath," I said, calling my higher Self in my meditation. "In fact, I refuse to die altogether just yet. I *choose* to live. If there's ever a moment when I needed you, this is it. Let's find a way, you and me. I know we can do it."

When I'd made that choice with such power, it interrupted all the other noise in my mind and allowed me to drop deeper into that place of silence where all seeds of creation exist. In that space, I reached out to my Inner Diamond. "Help me! Help me to conquer this and start anew."

About the Author

Born in the port town of Porbandar in Gujarat, India, my parents and I moved to London when I was ten. I studied in England, undertaking English, French and Politics at college. In a career spanning 25 years, I took on increasingly challenging responsibilities in the corporate world. One of my main roles was selling multimillion-dollar contracts into well-known global companies. Through the business I was in, I'm proud to have been one of the pioneers bringing India's Information Technology services into the heart of British and European companies.

Alongside my corporate career, I became a life coach and led personal transformation programmes to groups of hundreds at a time. As a freelance TV presenter, I interview *gurus*, entrepreneurs and politicians. A devoted practitioner, I'm also a certified *yoga* instructor.

I'm married and live in London.

Behind the Author

My birth town of Porbandar, a buzzing port along North West India's Arabian Sea coastline, is better known as the home of Mahatma Gandhi. I was brought up in a traditional Indian home with values rooted in ancient Vedic culture. We lived for most of my childhood close by the sea and some of my years were spent in a beautiful sea-facing house of my grandad's, a well-respected lawyer. As with many children in India, I was fortunate to have the influence of a grandmother who imbued in me the values of the age-old culture into which I was born. She encouraged me to read daily the *Bhagavad Gita* in Gujarati and to recite various Sanskrit *mantras* before I'd turned seven. This gave me a solid foundation on which to later build as I strived to heal the traumas of my past, and bring balance to a hectic life while working as a business executive with large global companies.

I loved my life in London and its flourishing entrepreneurial culture. Like a duck to water, I thrived on working internationally in hardcore business environments, selling leading-edge technology contracts to multi-national corporations. I am proud to have been one of the pioneers to convince large Western companies to start working with the Indian IT industry, which was growing in those days from its infancy into one of the largest parts of the Indian economy.

But at the same time, while working in the cut-throat world of business, I was fascinated by who we are deeper within. It was not long before I felt compelled to balance my professional corporate existence with, at the same time, finding a way to nourish my soul.

I yearned to experience more of the soulful, radiant inner being that I had seen glimpses of at various times in my life. During my holidays and sabbaticals, I travelled across India with *yogis* and *gurus* to see what more I could discover about the Self within. I pored over the *Vedas*, *Bhagavad Gita*, Shiva Sutras, the Puranas and Upanishads, soaking up whatever I could and went about applying some of these teachings to improve my quality of life, including in my work. Later in my quest, I travelled to many other places, including New Mexico, Hawaii and Kauai to seek out special people, places and answers to unresolved questions that throttled the possibility that life offered.

As my self-awareness grew, so did my desire to serve others. Alongside of my business life, when not travelling for work or meeting deadlines, I dedicated my weekends, holidays and any spare time over a number of years to become a life coach. I first followed a few years of hard training on how to help others in a responsible way to uncover their deepest issues and transform themselves. Then, I was allowed to go and assist in such programmes. It was not long before I had the privilege of leading these cutting-edge series of workshops myself, coaching large groups of 100 - 300 people at a time on how to deal more powerfully with the challenges of modern life and realise their goals and aspirations.

Yoga - the context for my life

As a child, I grew up watching my father regularly stand on his head for what seemed to me like hours. He was doing the Shirsasana *yoga* posture. Guided by his *guru*, the brilliant Sri Aurobindo, my father was an avid *yogi* who meditated regularly. Though Dad never taught me directly, simply watching him stand stock-still on his head and sit statuesque in deep, meditative immersions, captivated my imagination as a little girl. Around the age of twelve, I too started to attempt performing *yoga* postures. A few years later, I also began to meditate, purely guided by my intuitive inklings. On and off, I did *yoga* for twenty years but it was only when I stumbled into my first Vinyasa Flow training course did my *yoga* practise begin in earnest. This was with the extraordinary, internationally renowned *yoga* teacher, Shiva Rea. Her profound knowledge and approach to integrating the different aspects of *yoga* touched me deeply and inspired by Shiva, I took up training with her to be able to teach.

Other accomplished *yoga* masters of the Krishnamacharya lineage with whom I have studied include David Swenson, Richard Freeman, Ana Forrest, Anna Ashby, Hamish Hendry and Stewart Gilchrist. As well as Shiva Rea's Prana Flow Yoga, I also practise Mysore Style Ashtanga and other forms of dynamic yoga. I teach regularly and am committed to my daily practice.

Diving Deep

People and cultures fascinate me and I love exploring different parts of the world. My love of travel has taken me to swim with wild dolphins, exploring volcanoes, and visit temples, shrines and mystical places across the world.

I've studied several Indian and Buddhist spiritual systems and continue to delve into their richness to discover new facets of who we are. Unveiling the mysteries of the mind, spirit and what it means to be human excites me.

A keen diver, scuba diving satisfies my yearning for adventure and immersing into the unknown. The ocean can, at once, contain dangerous shipwrecks and beautiful reefs, treacherous sharks and playful dolphins.

For me, scuba diving offers a beautiful metaphor for diving into the deep ocean of the inner Self that can nourish the soul but also hold paradoxes, just like the many facets of our own beautiful being.

My years and years of soul searching have resulted in this, my first trilogy, *Karma & Diamonds*.

Karma & Diamonds

Book 1 - Moon Child

"One woman's journey from early trauma as a child in India to discovering the incredible power that lies inside us all."

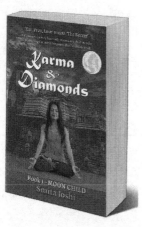

The young Smita lives with her family in Porbandar, Gandhi's coastal town in North West India. At the age of seven, a sudden shocking upheaval alters her view of life forever. This is just one of many traumatic events in her childhood. During these moments of crisis, she discovers a deep, mystical connection with the higher realms through her inner Self, which she calls her 'Inner Diamond'. She finds she has a natural ability to tap into the ancient wisdom of the Indian *gurus* purely by intuition.

When she is ten, her family moves to the UK. There, she grows into an enthusiastic adolescent but is quickly confronted with the challenge of trying to balance two very different cultures of modern-day London and a traditional Indian culture that has very specific plans for her. She struggles to find her place in the world, both physically and spiritually. Things culminate into a major crisis and she finds herself isolated.

Later, after college, there's the premature prospect of being married off quickly to a nice young man in India. She realises that this is not her destiny. She needs all her courage to try and make life work as an independent young woman. She learns the hard way and makes mistakes along the way during the start of her career, but eventually she pulls through and builds a life for herself, even managing to buy a flat at a young age.

She wonders why her life is such a constant struggle with no real prospect for inner peace and love, as she keeps on battling old traumas that have a tight grip on her, and that block her from getting close to others. The Inner Diamond shows her that she can only be free, fulfilled, and experience true love, if she can let go of the *karma* of past lives, of which she has seen glimpses through her young life. This inner wisdom tells her to leave everything behind and go on a quest to India. Trusting her inner Self because it has guided her well so far, she quits her job, rents out her flat, and leaves for India with no clue of where to go or what to do.

Karma & Diamonds

Book 3 - Diamond Revealed

"Will a life-threatening condition bring her quest to a premature end?"

Refusing to die, Smita calls once more onto her Inner Diamond to guide her. It takes her to the one doctor in the world who dares to operate on her.

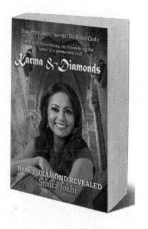

No sooner is she back from hospital that she sees an angel-bird in her meditation. It tells her the quest is not complete. More work is to be done and she is to go to Hawaii if she is to find freedom and fulfilment.

In Hawaii, reality and higher realms seem to merge as she witnesses many mystical events. On the volcano she meets the angel-bird again and he clears her path to encounter the goddess whom she has already encountered in her dreams.

She is taken to swim with wild dolphins in the ocean off the coast of Hawaii. They accept her into their pod and through their joyful leaf ritual, they grant her permission to be playful again.

She experiences a mysterious phenomenon at the stunning Shiva temple in Kauai, which the priests explain as a rare and precious blessing.

Loose ends still remain. When she returns back home, her intuition compels her to visit, in the nick of time, the one key person in her life with whom a significant completion must take place if she is to be at peace with her past.

This time, the cycles of *karma* seem finally complete and she can have an emotional reconciliation with her mother and those closest to her.

She is now liberated to soar at work and soon afterwards she meets a man who intrigues her. She certainly is ready for a beautiful partnership now. But will he capture her heart? Will she be able to find true love?